PRAISE FOR

YOGA AND SELF-ENQUIRY

We have arrived at a time of shared global crises and opportunities, a time that has been prophesied by spiritual communities and cultures around the world. The practices described in this timely book reflect ancient wisdom and are needed today like never before.
~ JOHN PERKINS, New York Times bestselling author

Lucy E. Johnson has written a classic. She tells us that her new book is meant to be a "practice manual for gaining direct Self-Knowledge." This is a high aspiration, and Johnson absolutely accomplishes her task. She guides the reader very precisely and methodically through a process of discernment developed over thousands of years by the most sophisticated masters of the yoga tradition. She does so without becoming bogged down in the sometimes incomprehensible welter of yoga metaphysics. Her guidance is exquisitely detailed, highly accurate, and profoundly practical and useful. I simply could not put this book down. Only a true practitioner of yoga, and one who is extremely knowledgeable about the breadth and depth of the yoga tradition, could have written this book. It is an awe-inspiring contribution. ~ STEPHEN COPE, bestselling author and Senior Scholar in Residence, Kripalu Center for Yoga and Health, Lenox MA, USA

Yoga and Self-Enquiry *is a book which you will not only want to keep by your bedside for ongoing study, inspiration, and guidance, but a book which you will also want to share with anyone you know, who is earnestly seeking the understanding and experience of the most satisfying and fulfilling answer to the question, "Who am I?"*
~ STEPHEN QUONG, Vedic Astrologer, California, USA

Steeped in yoga philosophy, Lucy Johnson draws upon traditional and key ancient yogic texts with expert skill as she blends and illuminates

other luminaries, inspiring the reader into contemplation. B.K.S Iyen-gar had photos of Śri Ramana Maharshi and Śri Ramakrishna on the walls of his own library – they were among his inspirational guidance for his teachings. ~ STÉPHANE N. LALO, Senior Iyengar Yoga Teacher, Iyengar Yoga Center of Marseille, France

Yoga and Self-Enquiry *is a uniquely successful attempt to take a highly complicated subject and hand it to the intelligent reader in a crisp, clear, and intriguing way. Seekers of Truth, lovers of philosophy, and all spiritual practitioners will find within this book practical guidance and stimulating teachings. This book is for you! Read it, practice what is taught, and see for yourself the power of this ancient knowledge.* ~ SWAMI KASHI MUKTANANDA SARASVATI, Uttarkashi, India

Here is a book that unveils the mysteries surrounding timeless philosophical truths that are expressed in two of the most prominent "doctrines" that we know: Patañjali's Raja Yoga and Jñāna Yoga (the path of knowledge). Lucy has created a bridge between the ideologies of mankind, and the means or practices, to incarnate these universal truths. She has made important Yoga theories accessible through precise exercises which are related to the texts quoted within the book. One cannot help but feeling the enthusiasm in Lucy's translations and citations. A book not only of facts, but also, of encouragement. Citations are an important practice in Yoga as they act as technical symbols that elevate the mind. If you find a citation you adhere to, read it again, contemplate on its meaning, and then put it into action. Enjoy.... ~ CHRISTOPHER STEPHENS, Yoga Acharya and founder of Madhura Yoga, France

Yoga and Self-Enquiry *is one of the best books I have ever read on the subject. The author breaks down complex ideas in a way that everyone can connect to. The exercises that put the teachings into action are both practical and provide a helpful means to apply yoga in your life and out into the world. Many realizations will be had if you read this book.* ~ LESLIE HOWARD, Yoga Therapist and Teacher

YOGA *and* Self-Enquiry

LUCY E. JOHNSON

YOGA AND SELF-ENQUIRY

by LUCY E. JOHNSON

lucyejohnson123@outlook.com

Copyright 2021 by Lucy E. Johnson

ISBN 978-82-303-5085-0

PERMISSIONS

Excerpts from *The Heart of Awareness: A Translation of the Ashtavakra Gita,* translated by Thomas Byrom. Copyright © 1990 by Thomas Byrom reprinted by arrangement with The Permissions Company, LLC on behalf of Shambhala Publications Inc., Boulder, Colorado, *shambhala.com.*

Excerpts from *Light on the Yoga Sutras of Patanjali* by B.K.S. Iyengar (Thorsons, New Edition 2002) reprinted by permission of HarperCollins Publishers Ltd.

DESIGN & TYPOGRAPHY

by D. Patrick Miller, Fearless Literary Services
www.fearlessbooks.com

FRONT COVER

The peepel tree, also known as the bodhi tree, is traditionally used as a metaphor of saṃsāra (the cycle of birth and death in the empirical universe). The tree of saṃsāra has its highest root above, in Brahman (God). Its seed is ignorance (avidyā) of one's true nature, which is Pure Consciousness. Of this tree it is said:

"Buddhi [intellect] is its trunk, the sense-openings are its hollows, the great elements its boughs, the sense-objects its leaves and branches, Dharma and Adharma (virtue and vice) its beautiful flowers, pleasure and pain its fruits. Having cut asunder this tree with the powerful sword of knowledge of the Self, and then having attained to the eternal bliss of Brahman, no one comes back from there again." ~ SWAMI SIVANANDA

TABLE OF CONTENTS

FOREWORD

IN THE heart of all human beings abides the voice of the conscience. Its function is to discriminate the wrong from the right, the impure from the pure, the unpleasant from the pleasant and the impermanent from the eternal. Almost everyone can hear this voice, yet in order to avoid our weaknesses and for the purpose of our personal comfort we try not to listen to it, or to interpret its advice, or to promise ourselves that it is the last experience or last time that we don't follow its advice. In Hindu Philosophy this voice is called "Dharmendriya" or the organ of righteousness. The aim of the Hindu Spiritual Quest is to trace, to awaken, to tune this voice of dharma and to develop the required inner strength to listen to its indications and to follow its instructions.

I feel privileged having been one of the first readers of Lucy Johnson's *Yoga and Self-Enquiry*. I met Lucy some years ago in a workshop and noted very quickly her disciplined spirit and her devotional approach towards the spiritual quest and the practice of yoga. I felt that she was not a type of student to remain content with a gymnastic approach to yoga positions. She continued with a deep urge to learn and to study Indian Philosophy and the theory behind the practice of yoga. Now, in these pages which lay in front of us, she offers with a great clarity and true generosity the fruits of her long years of research work.

Yoga, like other schools of Hindu philosophy (sad-darśanas) belongs to thirty-two primary vidyās (knowledges). Yet one of the main differences between yoga and other darśanas is that yoga is the only one with a practice.

The theory of yoga has been codified and systematised by the great sage Patañjali around 400 years B.C. Patañjali was not the inventor of yoga. We know that yoga had existed before him and his great work was to create a synthesis of the existing knowledge and information, putting it under the form of 195 aphorisms (sūtras), which may be considered as a precise road-map for a spiritual seeker in yoga.

Through the study of these aphorisms we note that Patañjali is the first and last who could put the mechanism of the human mind under the form of mathematical formulas. All others, before or after him, had to use metaphors and even stories to convey their teachings.

The study and understanding of Yoga Sūtras is not a very easy task. From the very beginning of our eras many yogis and philosophers have tried to comment upon it. The most famous one is that of Vyāsa which is almost inseparable from the text. In traditional study, this commentary is studied before the text itself. To my knowledge there are about twenty-six classical commentaries on yoga-sūtra.

Traditionally, it is believed that yoga is 99% practice and only 1% theory. My revered Guruji, Yogacharya B.K.S. Iyengar, used to tell us that even that 1% could be understood through the practice.

Another well-known school of Hindu Philosophy is Vedānta. Vedānta itself has seven schools, the most famous one being Advaīta of Ādi Śankara. In this book, Lucy Johnson has successfully tried, following the examples of Swami Vivekananda and Swami Sivananda, to bring the practice of yoga and Śankar Vedānta closer to each other.

Along with her clear explanations and practical exercises she creates a joyful urge and enthusiasm in the reader to take up a serious practice of the subject.

There is a beautiful quotation in Viṣṇu Purāṇa that sage Vyāsa includes in his commentary on yoga sūtras:

"Yoga is the teacher of Yoga; Yoga is to be understood through Yoga. Live in Yoga to realise Yoga; comprehend Yoga through Yoga; he who is free from distractions enjoys Yoga through Yoga".

I wish this book and its author the full and well-deserved success that they merit.

SRICHARAN FAEQ BIRIA, PHD
Paris, 30th March 2021

ACKNOWLEDGMENTS

Firstly, I would like to express my gratitude to Michael Langford, the author of *The Most Direct Means to Internal Bliss*, for pointing me with utmost clarity towards my own true nature.

A deep heartfelt thanks to the Chinmaya International Foundation for their authentic teaching programs in Vedānta and Sanskrit.

I am forever indebted to the tremendous contributions by the following and their associated work: *The Yoga Sūtras of Patañjali* by Edwin F. Bryant; *Light on the Yoga Sūtras of Patañjali* by B.K.S. Iyengar; and *Raja Yoga* by Swami Sivananda.

Thank you to Swami Kashi (*www.heartpilgrim.org*) for his willingness to look at my initial draft and his thoughtful observations.

Thank you to Swami Sarvapriyananda (current spiritual leader of the Vedānta Society of New York) for his wonderfully accessible teachings of classic Vedāntic texts such as Dṛg-Dṛśya-Viveka and Aparokṣānubhūti.

My gratitude also goes to Swami Dayatmananda (previous spiritual leader of Ramakrishna-Vedānta Centre, U.K.) for his lectures on both Patañjali yoga sutras and Vedānta, which draw from the teachings and lives of Śri Ramakrishna, Śri Sarada Devi and Swami Vivekananda.

Finally, a big thank you to all the wonderful yoga teachers I have been fortunate to study with and learn from over the years. With a special thanks to Constance Braden of the Houston Iyengar Yoga Studio who gave me my first introduction to Patañjali's yoga sūtras.

DEDICATION

*To my husband Kårstein
and daughters Sophie and
Isabel*

Transliteration* and Pronunciation Guide

VOWELS

a	fun	ḷ	like "lree"
ā	car	ḹ	same as ḷ but held twice as long
i	pin	e	play
ī	feet	ai	high
u	put	o	over
ū	pool	au	cow
ṛ	rig	aṃ	umbrella
ṝ	reach	aḥ	ahoy

CONSONANTS

ka	kind	da	date
kha	blockhead	dha	kindhearted
ga	gate	na	numb
gha	Log-hut	pa	purse
ṅa	sing	pha	sapphire
ca	chunk	ba	but
cha	match	bha	abhor
ja	jug	ma	mother
jha	hedgehog	ya	young
ña	bunch	ra	run
ṭa	touch	la	luck
ṭha	ant-hill	va	virtue
ḍa	duck	śa	shove
ḍha	godhood	ṣa	bushel
ṇa	thunder	sa	sir
ta	take	ha	house
tha	fainthearted	kṣa	worksheet
		tra	trap
		jña	"j-nya"

*Based on the International Alphabet of Sanskrit Transliteration (IAST)

PART 1

SELF-ENQUIRY

*"Whatever be the means adopted, you must at last return
to the Self; so why not abide in the Self here and now?"*
~ Śri Ramana Maharshi [1]

Dear reader and fellow yogi,

In this book I aim to share with you a fresh look at Patañjali's Eight Limbs of Yoga as a direct means to Self-knowledge. By the term Self, I refer to your true essence. The goal of Self-knowledge is final liberation: an end to the cycle of birth and death for which various names are given including emancipation, kaivalya, mokṣa, nirvāṇa, or Self-realization.

You will come to understand firsthand that you do not have to wait until you are Self-realized to know the Self or God. If you give Yoga and Self-enquiry a good try, you will know the Self as a constant living presence, not just as a lofty, philosophical ideal to be actualized at some time in the future.

Not only that, your yoga practice will take on a deeper meaning and your everyday life will flow with greater ease by being connected to the infinite wisdom within. As Swami Vivekananda said:

*"If the Student thinks he is the Spirit, he will be a better
Student. If the Lawyer thinks he is the Spirit, he will be a
better Lawyer, and so on."*

Yoga, like all spiritual endeavors, begins with an inner longing to find meaning and happiness in life and reduce suffering. In yoga sūtra 2.4, Patañjali tells us that it is the lack of knowledge of one's true identity that is the source of all worldly suffering:

"Lack of true knowledge is the source of all pains and sorrows whether dormant, attenuated, interrupted or fully active." [2]

We mistakenly think that we are limited, separate individuals rather than the One-Eternal-Infinite Spirit that we truly are. This constitutes spiritual ignorance (avidyā) which keeps us in the cycle of birth and death (saṃsāra).

Invested in this mistaken notion of individual personhood, we seek happiness externally while simultaneously trying to avoid everything that threatens pain. Our attractions and aversions lead to a mix of consequences. This process is commonly referred to as the wheel of karma, mentioned in the Bṛhadāraṇyaka Upaniṣad:

"And here they say that a person consists of desires,
and as is his desire, so is his will;
and as is his will, so is his deed;
and whatever deed he does, that he will reap."
~ Verses IV.iv.5-IV.iv.6

If spiritual ignorance is the fundamental cause of suffering, the remedy is removal of ignorance through knowledge of what we truly are. This can only be brought about by investigation into our true nature, which we identify as "Self-enquiry" (vichāra). The path of knowledge is also traditionally referred to as jñāna yoga.

The importance of Self-Knowledge is discussed in the Yoga-tattva Upaniṣad, one of the oldest yoga texts:

"I relate to you the means to be employed for destruction of errors:

Without the practice of yoga, how could knowledge set the Ātman (Self) free?

Inversely, how could the practice of yoga alone, devoid of knowledge, succeed in the task?

The seeker of Liberation must direct his energies to both simultaneously.

The source of unhappiness lies in Ajñāna (ignorance);

Knowledge alone sets one free. This is a dictum found in all Vedas." ~ Verses 14-16

In Aparokṣānubhūti, a text attributed to Ādi Śaṅkarācārya, Self-enquiry is defined as an investigation along the lines of:

"Who am I? How is this world created? Who is its creator? Of what material is this world made? This is the way of that Vichāra."

"I am neither the body, a combination of the five elements of matter, nor am I an aggregate of the senses; I am something different from these. This is the way of that Vichāra."

"Everything is produced by ignorance, and dissolves in the wake of Knowledge. The various thoughts must be the creator. Such is this Vichāra."

"The material cause of these two (i.e. ignorance and thought) is the One (without a second), subtle (not apprehended by the senses) and unchanging Sat (Existence), just as the earth is the material (cause) of the pot and the like. This is the way of that Vichāra."

"As I am also the One, the Subtle, the Knower, the Witness, the Ever-Existent and the Unchanging, so there is no doubt that I am 'That'. Such is this enquiry." ~ Verses 12-16

Thus, Self-enquiry is the process by which we uncover our real, inward Self and then turn our attention toward it.

Swami Venkatesananda, in his translation of the classic text Yoga Vāsiṣṭha explains:

> *"Vichāra has been translated 'enquiry' or Self-enquiry'. It should not be confused with intellectual analysis. It is **direct observation** or '**looking within**'."* [3]

Part 1 of this book will lead you step by step through the process of Self-enquiry using a combination of simple, powerful contemplation and visualization exercises.

> **"There is a universal reality in ourselves that aligns us with a universal reality that is everywhere."**
>
> ~ B.K.S. Iyengar [4]

The exercises are presented to enable the first-hand acquirement of knowledge. I recommend that you carry out the exercises in the order that they are presented, as they build on each other.

In Part 2, the insights gained will be deepened and assimilated through the practice of Patañjali's eight limbs of yoga. It is only through direct experience that any doubts may be removed.

Part 2 will present methods for meditation on the Self. Swami Vidyāraṇya, the author of Pañcadaśī (a 14th-century text on Vedānta), writes:

> *"To reach treasures deeply hidden in the earth, there is nothing for it but to dig. **So to have direct knowledge of Me, the Self, there is no other means than meditation on one's Self**".* ~ Verse IX.153

Thus "knowledge" signifies more than just intellectual understanding. This book is meant to be a 'practice manual' for gaining direct Self-knowledge, which Patañjali clarifies in yoga sūtra 1.49:

"This truth-bearing knowledge and wisdom is distinct from and beyond the knowledge gleaned from books, testimony, or inference." [5]

The glorious result is described in yoga sūtra 2.25:

*"The destruction of ignorance **through right knowledge** breaks the link binding the Seer to the seen*. This is Kaivalya, emancipation."* [6]

*Seer is another name used for the Self. "The Seer and the Seen" is the title of the first Self-enquiry exercise given in Chapter 1.

A Brief History of Knowledge

Advaita Vedānta is a non-dual teaching which traces its roots to the oldest Upaniṣads or ancient Sanskrit texts from India. If the term 'non-dual' is unfamiliar, its meaning will become clear in these pages. I have provided English translations for Sanskrit terms.

The most prominent exponent of Advaita Vedānta is considered to be Ādi Śaṅkarācārya, born in India around the 8th century. In addition to his own works, he commented on some of the Upaniṣads and other scriptures including the Bhagavad Gītā, and possibly the Yoga Sūtras of Patañjali. Ādi Śaṅkarācārya founded ten monastic orders, one of which was the Saraswati lineage.

Recently prominent in the Sarawasti lineage was Swami Sivananda (1887 to 1963), of Rishikesh, India, who devoted his life to the practice and propagation of Yoga and Vedānta*. For quotes in this book, I have drawn on the teachings of Swami Sivananda, in addition to others such as Śri Ramana Maharshi (1879 to 1950).

*Whenever I use the term 'Vedānta', I am always referring specifically to Advaita Vedānta and not to any of the other schools of Vedānta such as the Dvaita Vedānta (dualism school) of Madhvācārya or Viśiṣṭādvaita Vedānta (qualified non-dualism school) of Rāmānuja.

Śri Ramana Maharshi was an Indian Saint who recommended the use of Self-enquiry to achieve mokṣa (Self-realization or final liberation). Of Śri Ramana Maharshi, Swami Sivananda said:

"Ramana was a living example of the teaching of the Upaniṣads. His life was at once the message and the philosophy of his teachings. He spoke to the hearts of men.

The great Maharshi found Himself within himself and then gave out to the world the grand but simple message of his great life, 'Know Thyself'." ~ In his book *Lives of Saints*

Last but by no means least, we have the Yoga Sūtras of Patañjali. The yoga sutras, compiled by the great sage Patañjali some 2000 or more years ago, provide us with the path of Rāja yoga — the science of concentration and meditation. The yoga sūtras were first introduced to the West by Swami Vivekananda in the late 19ᵗʰ century. We will be viewing the practice of yoga through the lens of Advaita Vedānta.

Now, as you are about to begin….

You are about to dive deep into Svādhyāya — the study or enquiry that leads to knowledge of the Self.

The first five chapters are at the very heart of Self-enquiry. You will discover later in Part 2, that Svādhyāya is not only one of the niyamas (self-disciplines) but designated by Patañjali as an 'act of yoga'. This is for the simple reason that without knowing the Self how can one become permanently established in the Self?

I strongly encourage you, therefore, to use the text and exercises in the forthcoming chapters as a practical means for direct and engaged observation. This is the 'direct observation' or 'looking within' referred to earlier in this section.

I also gently recommend that any notion you may have that

what is being described here is theory and not so relevant to your day-to-day practice of yoga be laid aside. The background theory given is there primarily to help your understanding.

With this, I wish you good luck as you now proceed!

CHAPTER 1

The Seer and the Seen

*"The Self can be known immediately. The Self is ever present.
On account of ignorance, and on account of the combination of the
body and the senses, people do not know the Self either in the waking
or in the dream state." ~ Ādi Śaṅkarācārya* [7]

*"Men go abroad to wonder at the heights of mountains, at the huge
waves of the sea, at the long courses of the rivers, at the vast compass
of the ocean, at the circular motions of the stars, and they pass by
themselves without wondering."*
~ Saint Augustine

THE FIRST Self-enquiry exercise is based on the very first verse of Dṛg-Dṛśya-Viveka, commonly attributed to Bhārati Tirtha from the 14th century.

> *"The Truth is that the Self is constant and unintermittent Awareness."*
>
> ~ Śri Ramana Maharshi [8]

*"The form (object) is perceived and the eye is its perceiver.
It (eye) is perceived and the mind is its perceiver.* **The mind
with its modifications is perceived and the Witness
(the Self) is verily the perceiver.** *But It (the Witness) is
not perceived (by any other)."*

Put simply:

The Self (Puruṣa) is your continuous background of awareness — the unchanging Witness.

In yoga sūtra 4.18, it is explained:

"The modifications of the mind are always known to the Self due to the unchanging nature of Puruṣa." [9]

We do not notice the background of awareness because we are habitually tangled up in mental activity.

Other terms for the Self which you may come across include: Puruṣa*; Ātman; Brahman; Sat-Cit-Ānanda (Existence-Consciousness-Bliss); Sākṣī (Witness); Draṣṭā (Seer); I AM; Turīya; Presence; Pure Consciousness; Pure Awareness; Beingness; and Spirit.

*In these pages, Puruṣa is defined as consciousness in accordance with the yoga system.

Please familiarize yourself with these terms. Some of them will be clarified in their proper context later. However, it is important to know that they are all pointers to the same Pure Consciousness (or Pure Awareness) that you are in truth.

> *"Discrimination between the 'seer' and the 'seen' is the road leading to the realization of the Truth."*
>
> ~ Swami Sivananda [10]

Next, I would like to introduce you to the first exercise.

The main principle in this exercise is that anything you perceive (observe) or know as an object cannot be you.

Three important points to assimilate in Exercise 1 are:

1) The Self is not something far away and hard to find. It is your normal background of awareness that is there all the time — your everyday consciousness that is looking at this page **right now.**

2) The Self is not a thought construct; it is that which is aware of thoughts. Thoughts come and go, but awareness is continuous.

3) The Self is your inner quiet center.

Exercise 1: **The Seer and the Seen**

<table>
<tr><td colspan="2" align="center">Step 1: "The form (object) is perceived and the eye is its perceiver."</td></tr>
<tr><td>

Look at a chosen object in front of you, for example, a pen or a cup.

Be aware of yourself observing the object with the eyes. Confirm as a fact to yourself that:

Perceiver = eyes
Perceived = object (pen, cup etc)

</td><td>

<u>Hints</u>
This step is relatively quick, requiring just a few seconds to acknowledge that your eyes are perceiving (observing) the object. Your eyes, therefore, are different from the object.

</td></tr>
</table>

<table>
<tr><td colspan="2" align="center">Step 2: "It (eye) is perceived and the mind is its perceiver."</td></tr>
<tr><td>

Close your eyes and notice that the mind is aware (perceives or observes) that the eyes are now closed. That is, the mind "knows" the condition of the eyes.

Take the time you need to confirm that:

Perceiver = mind
Perceived = eyes

</td><td>

<u>Hints</u>
Although your mind does not "see" it is aware of the state of the eyes. For example, the mind knows if the eyes are closed or if there are other eye-related conditions, such as not being able to see long distances. We can conclude that the mind perceives the eyes and is therefore different from the eyes.

</td></tr>
</table>

Step 3: ***"The mind with its modifications is perceived and the Witness (the Self) is verily the perceiver."***

For this step it also helps to close the eyes. Take the time you need. Bring a thought in to the mind such as: *"My eyes are closed; I no longer see any object".* Now, notice that which is aware or witnesses (observes) this thought. **Perceiver: SELF** **Perceived: thought(s)** **i.e. mind**	<u>Hints</u> The background of awareness witnessing or observing the thought is the constant and unchanging SELF. As soon as you carry out this Step you are abiding in the Self. **The Self is different from thoughts and memories — it is that which is *aware* of thoughts and memories.** **The Self is different from emotions and feelings — it is that which is *aware* of emotions and feelings.**

Step 4: ***"But It (the Witness) is not perceived (by any other)."***

Investigate as a fact for yourself that there is nothing else that perceives the witness investigated in Step 3. That is, there is no other awareness outside this awareness.

We can conclude, therefore, that the Self cannot be known as an object of perception — it is the ultimate subject.*

*In his commentary on the Yoga Sūtras, Śri Vyāsa refers to Puruṣa as "buddhi-bodhātmān", which may be translated as: the knower of all thought.

Pause for Reflection

Sit quietly for a few minutes. Bring your attention to your awareness that is looking out through your eyes right now at this page or the space around you.

Now close your eyes and observe that the same awareness that was looking out at the room just a moment ago is still there.

Notice that your awareness is constant, unchanging and always present. It is never not there.

Now you have completed the first exercise....

You will undoubtedly find that these methods/exercises require self-effort and focused concentration. The benefit of this, however, is that it slows down your pace of reading considerably. You cannot rush this process! You may even find yourself re-visiting these early chapters later to consolidate your experiential knowledge and understanding.

I ask only that you give it your best shot! In Part 2, things will get lighter again as we move into more familiar territory — the eight limbs of yoga.

You will also notice that several boxed quotes are included throughout each of the chapters, in addition to the stand-alone quotes given at the beginning of each chapter. These are provided to encourage contemplation on your behalf, which is an integral part of Svādhyāya (self-study/enquiry). If a certain quote does not resonate with you, or you have difficulty understanding its relevance, please continue with the main text.

CHAPTER 2

Enquiry into the Five Sheaths

"My Child,
Because you think you are the body,
For a long time you have been bound.
Know you are pure awareness.
With this knowledge as your sword
Cut through your chains.
And be happy!"
~ Aṣṭāvakra Gītā[11]

"Don't you know that you yourselves are God's temple
and that God's Spirit dwells in your midst?"
~ 1 Corinthians 3:16

THE AIM of Exercise 1 was to reintroduce you to your true Self — the awareness 'behind' all thought or mental activity. If someone were to ask "Who are you?" your first response would probably be "I am John/Susan", referring to yourself as an individual with unique characteristics — a physical body and accompanying personality.

There are several ways to demonstrate why your real identity cannot be the body or mind. Some of these are presented in the following exercise, which uses the model of the five sheaths (kośas) to describe the body/mind complex. This model is said to originate from the Taittirīya Upaniṣad. The sheaths are so-called because they appear to "cover" the Self or Ātman.

The importance of Self-enquiry using the five sheaths is emphasized in Ātma-bodha, a small Sanskrit text (translated as "Self-Knowledge") attributed to Ādi Śaṅkarācārya, in which it is said:

"One should, through discrimination, separate the pure
and inmost Self from the sheaths by which It is covered,
as one separates a rice-kernel from the covering husk
by striking it with a pestle." ~ Verse 15

Another common way in yoga of classifying the body/mind complex is as three bodies: gross (physical); subtle (or astral) and causal. The three bodies are also indicated in the table so it can be understood how they relate to the five sheaths.

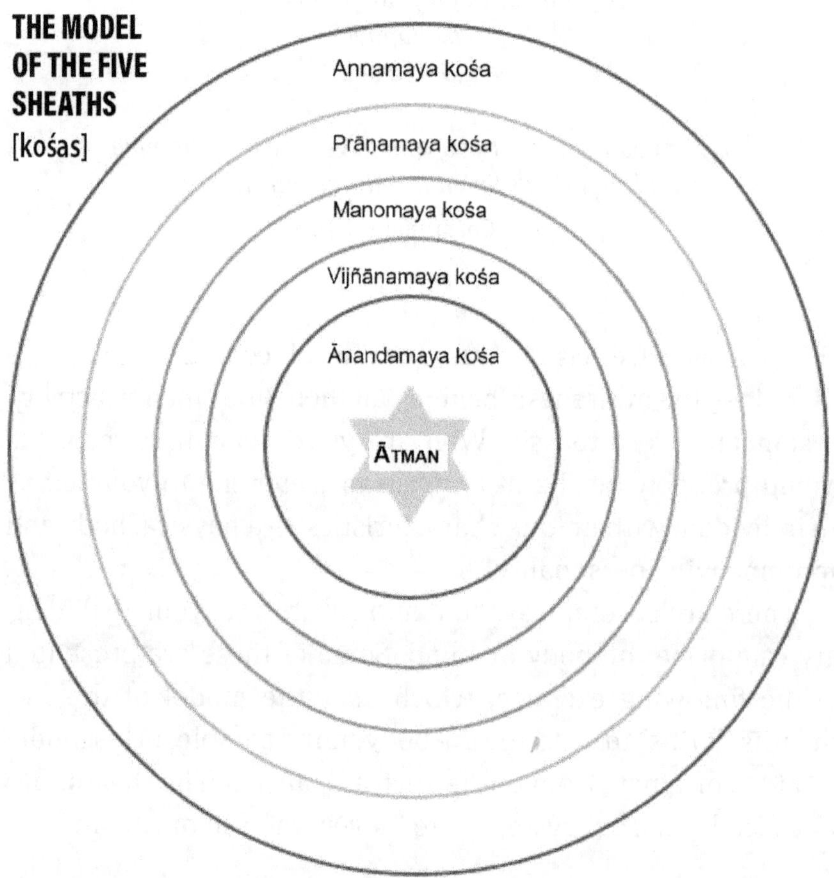

Kośa (sheath)	Description	Three Bodies Classification
Annamaya kośa Food Sheath ('Anna' literally means food.)	The physical body nourished by the food we eat. It consists of muscles, bones, tissue, organs etc.	**Sthūla śarīra –** Gross or physical body Equivalent to the outermost sheath: annamaya kośa.
Prāṇamaya kośa Vital (life) force or energy sheath	Made up of prāṇa which is the life force in the body and manifests physically as the breath. We experience the prāṇamaya kośa when we feel, for example, energized, sleepy, hungry and thirsty. Prāṇa is named in accordance with its five functions: Prāṇa — Respiration Apāna — Expulsion Samāna — Digestion Vyāna — Circulation Udāna — Vomiting	**Sūkṣma śarīra –** Subtle (astral) body Equivalent to the sum of: prāṇamaya, manomaya, and vijñānamaya kośas.
Manomaya kośa Mind sheath	Corresponds to the mind/mental activity. It is the part of the mind that registers the impressions from our sensory apparatus (eyes, nose, ears, etc) in addition to our basic experience of mental activity including our emotions.	
Vijñānamaya kośa Intellect sheath	Corresponds to our experience of intellect, problem solving, intuition and insight. Its qualities include discrimination, and decision making.	
Ānandamaya kośa Bliss sheath	Also called the causal body, because although bodiless, it is the cause or seed of the other bodies/sheaths. The ānandamaya kośa originates with ignorance of one's real identity as Ātman (the Self or Pure Consciousness). It contains the impressions of experience (karmic imprints) as a result of past experiences from current and previous lives.	**Kāraṇa śarīra -** Causal body Equivalent to the innermost sheath: ānandamaya kośa.

EXERCISE 2: **Enquiry into the Five Sheaths**

In this exercise, you will use three distinguishing features of the Self to investigate whether your true identity can be found in one or more of the five sheaths (comprising the body and mind complex). The three features are:

i.   The Self (witness consciousness) is constant/unchanging*
ii. There is only one Self
iii. The Self is the Perceiver **

*This is not a philosophical statement. If you turn your attention to the background of awareness and observe it steadily, you will recognize that it is constant/unchanging.

**Everything that is known to you is an object and must therefore be different to you, the conscious observer (perceiver).

For each sheath, you will consider each of the three features listed above and investigate (through contemplation) whether they also apply to the sheath. If not, the sheath must be different from the Self.

The method for carrying out Exercise 2 is to read and contemplate the comparisons between the Self and corresponding sheath (given in the three columns), going deeper each time as you progress to the next sheath.

As you have discovered in Exercise 1, the Self is the background of awareness — the Witness of all thought. As you carry out the following exercise, try to bring your attention to your awareness, and **from this centre** contemplate the various comparisons given.

Annamaya kośa - Physical sheath		
The Self is constant/ unchanging *Your body is constantly changing. It is subject to birth, growth, decay and death.* *Yet you know yourself to be the same person that you were when you were a baby, small child, teenager, etc. This is because the witnessing consciousness within (the Self) does not change.*	**There is only one Self** *Your body consists of many parts such as: arms, legs, internal organs, etc.*	**The Self is the Perceiver** *Your physical body is an object of your perception. You can see, touch, taste, smell and hear it.* *Whereas the Self, the ultimate Subject, is not an object of perception. It is not possible to see, touch, taste, smell or hear the Self.*

You are not the physical body – now go deeper!

<table>
<tr><td colspan="3">Prāṇamaya kośa - Vital (life) force or energy sheath</td></tr>
<tr>
<td>The Self is constant/unchanging</td>
<td>There is only one Self</td>
<td>The Self is the perceiver</td>
</tr>
<tr>
<td>The life force in your body is constantly changing. Throughout the day you experience different energy levels within the body. One moment you may feel sleepy, and alert the next.</td>
<td>Although there is only one Prāṇa, it is classified into the five vāyus (winds) each with a different function (see table above), location and energetic quality.</td>
<td>You perceive (observe) if you are tired, hungry, sleepy, etc. You also clearly observe the breath. The life force (prāṇa) is therefore different to the Self.</td>
</tr>
</table>

You are not the prāṇa (life force) – now go deeper!

<table>
<tr><td colspan="3">Manomaya kośa - Mind sheath</td></tr>
<tr>
<td>The Self is constant/ unchanging</td>
<td>There is only one Self</td>
<td>The Self is the perceiver</td>
</tr>
<tr>
<td>Your mental state is constantly changing. You may be happy one moment, sad the next. Memories, desires, thoughts, and feelings come and go in a never-ending flux.</td>
<td>You experience the mind as many thoughts in addition to the various functions of the mind, such as reception of sensory data, emotional responses, etc.</td>
<td>You are aware of thoughts, mental images, feelings, emotions, and desires as they arise. These are all objects of knowledge. The Self, therefore, is different from the mind.</td>
</tr>
</table>

You are not the mind – now go deeper!

<table>
<tr><th colspan="3" align="center">Vijñānamaya kośa- Intellect sheath</th></tr>
<tr><td>The Self is constant/ unchanging

Your intellect, problem solving abilities, etc are constantly changing and evolving.</td><td>There is only one Self

There are many different aspects to your overall intelligence including spatial, analytical, and linguistic intelligence.</td><td>The Self is the perceiver

You are aware of your efforts to understand problems or figure out solutions. The intellect is an object of your awareness.

The Self is therefore different from the intellect.</td></tr>
</table>

You are not the intellect – now go deeper!

<table>
<tr><th align="center">Ānandamaya kośa - Bliss sheath</th></tr>
<tr><td>

The ānandamaya kośa is also an object of your experience. To understand this, it is necessary to consider your experience of deep sleep.

Deep sleep is a state devoid of thoughts and sense perceptions as the mind (plus intellect) and senses are shutdown. You are not aware of the physical body (as an object of your perception). Yet you, the consciousness (or awareness), remains. After waking up from deep sleep one's sense is that we slept soundly and knew nothing. Deep sleep is an experience of the absence of objects.

This is the subject of the following quote:

"Ignorance of objects is the object of awareness in deep sleep. The awareness of the objects in the waking and dream and the awareness of the lack of objects in deep sleep is the same". ~ Pañcadaśī (Verse I.6)

The Self, therefore, must be other than the bliss sheath.

</td></tr>
</table>

You are not even the bliss sheath – go deeper still!

What is left after negating the sheaths?

The answer is Silence.

Silence is another name for the Self (Ātman) — the Witness (that which is aware) of the five sheaths. The sheaths, which are inert, are illumined by the presence of the Ātman.

In the above Self-enquiry exercise, you went increasingly deeper within to discover your Self — that which cannot be experienced as an object.

We can see from Exercise 2 why the system of sheaths is referred to poetically as a 'cave' in the Kaṭha Upaniṣad:

"Realizing through self-contemplation that the Ātman, difficult to be seen, deeply hidden, situated in the cave (of the heart), dwelling in the depth, the wise-one leaves behind both joy and sorrow." ~ Verse I.ii.12

Interestingly, Meister Eckhart, the 13th century German Christian mystic, used strikingly Vedāntic language based on his own intuitive experience:

"A human being has so many skins inside, covering the depths of the heart. We know so many things, but we don't know ourselves! Why, thirty or forty skins or hides, as thick and hard as an ox's or bear's, cover the soul. Go into your own ground and learn to know yourself there."

Pause for Reflection

In Exercise 2, the Self was described as:

- Constant/unchanging
- One (without parts)
- Cannot be perceived as an object

Reflect on the above as you bring your attention to your Self — the witness consciousness or background of awareness.

Take a few minutes now to observe both your physical body and mind (thoughts).

Automatically a gap is introduced between You (the Self) and the body and mind, both of which are objects of your awareness.

The Nature of One's Soul

At some point during the Self-enquiry process, you may ask: "Where does my soul come in to all this?" We experience ourselves to be a separate individual with a body and unique personality, the Sanskrit term for which is jiva.

We owe our personality to our subtle body,* which upon death separates from the physical body and continues (transmigrates), along with the causal body, to the next incarnation.

*The mind and intellect (part of the subtle body) are the very substance or fabric of one's personality. They are dependent upon one's inherent and innate tendencies or inclinations, also called vāsanās. The seat of the vāsanās is the causal body.

Exercise 2 demonstrates that the five sheaths (or corresponding three bodies) cannot be the Self (Ātman). The Ātman is one's real Soul, the nature of which is described in the Tejobindu Upaniṣad:

> *"I am of the nature of consciousness.*
> *I am made of consciousness and bliss.*
> *I am non-dual, pure in form, absolute knowledge,*
> *absolute love.*
> *I am changeless, devoid of desire or anger,*
> *I am detached.*
> *I am One Essence, un-limitedness, utter consciousness.*
> *I am boundless Bliss, existence and transcendent Bliss.*
> *I am the Ātman, that revels in itself.*
> *I am the Saccidānanda* that is eternal, enlightened*
> *and pure."* ~ Verses III.1-12

*A compound Sanskrit word made up of: Sat = Existence; Cit = Consciousness; ānanda = Bliss

The Self (Ātman) is eternal. In the Bhagavad Gītā, Lord Krishna tells us:

"It is not born, nor does It ever die; after having been, it again ceases not to be; unborn, eternal, changeless and ancient, it is not killed when the body is killed." ~ Verse 2.20

There is only one Self* that illumines the mind of all beings. Lord Krishna also goes on to say:

"I am the Self, dwelling in the heart of all beings, and the beginning, the middle, and the end of all that lives as well."
~ Bhagavad Gītā (Verse 10.20)

*Sāṁkhya (the theoretical foundation and sister philosophy to yoga) is said to uphold many Puruṣas. This is a matter of perspective rather than a contradiction and will be clarified in a later chapter.

The Self — Finding the Missing Gold Necklace

The purpose of Self-enquiry is to intuit the Self or Ātman. Nobody can do that for us. There should be an 'aha!' moment of sudden insight upon discovering that the Ātman is not something we have to strive to obtain, but is 'closer than the closest', our very own Self!

A traditional Vedāntic metaphor used to describe this is that of the 'missing' gold necklace, described in the following quote by Swami Sivananda:

"A person wears round his neck a gold necklace and in excitement and confusion searches here and there. He walks and runs this side and that side but nowhere does he find the necklace, though it is around his own neck. Similarly, the individual or the jiva searches for Perfection and Bliss outside, everywhere, forgetting the fact that the Immortal Seat or Ātman is its very being itself and that it is identical with that Brahman."* [12]

*Brahman is Reality or God (to be further clarified in a later chapter).

The greatness of Self-knowledge is also expressed in the Kena Upaniṣad:

"If one would know (It) here, then there is the true end (of all aspirations). If one would not know (It) here, then great is the loss (for him). Knowing (It) in every single being, the wise, on departing from this world, become Immortal." ~ Verse II.5

Warning!

In this chapter, through direct observation, you have enquired into the nature of the physical body in addition to the mind and intellect. All of which are objects of your awareness and therefore not the Self — the true You.

In the next chapter our focus will now be entirely on the mind/intellect. It is not uncommon at this stage to experience some mental resistance, if you haven't already. After all, it is the mind/intellect that we tend to identity with the most, even more so than the physical body.

If you experience some resistance, my advice is that you proceed slowly — try not to cover a lot of material in one sitting.

CHAPTER 3

Enquiry into the Ego

"The I thought is said to be the sum total of all thoughts.
The source of the I thought has to be enquired into."
~ Sri Ramana Gita (VII.3-7)

I N THE previous chapter, you hopefully reached the understanding that your true identity is not the body nor the mind/intellect, but the Ātman (Self).

However, in daily life we have a strong habit of identifying with body, mind and intellect through the use of the term "I" (and "me"

> **"'This is he,'**
> **'I am this,'**
> **'That is mine,'**
> **Such ideas constitute**
> **the mind;**
> **It disappears**
> **When one ponders over**
> **these false ideas."**
>
> ~ Yoga-Vāsiṣṭha

or "mine") together with an infinite combination of words such as "I like this"; "I am doing such and such today"; "it is mine"; etc.

What or who exactly is this 'I'?

"I" (and "me"/"mine") represents our false identity as a separate individual. It is the 'little self'. This 'I' is also referred to as the 'I-thought' or 'ego' (ahaṁkāra or asmitā).

Yet the ego is only a thought construct or idea. We can clearly observe (witness) the thought "I am the body", just as we witness any other thought.

As the I-thought is an object of our awareness, it cannot be the Self.

Please slowly contemplate the following quote by Śri Ramana Maharshi:

"The Self is Pure Consciousness.

Yet the man identifies himself with the body which is itself insentient and does not say 'I am the body' of its own accord. Someone else says so. The unlimited Self does not. Who else is he that says so?

A spurious 'I' arises between the Pure Consciousness and the insentient body and imagines itself limited to the body.

Seek this and it will vanish as a phantom.

That phantom is the ego, or the mind or the individuality". [13]

That which we call our mind consists only of thoughts — the words or mental pictures in our head at any given moment. Even if a thought does not contain "I" it arises due to our sense of individuality (asmitā): our belief that we are a separate body and mind. This is described in yoga sūtra 4.4:

"Constructed or created mind springs from the sense of individuality (asmitā)".[14]

"Don't be interested in the words that the mind is serving up for you. It is putting them there to tempt you into a stream of thoughts that will take you away from the Self. You have to ignore them all and focus on the light that is shining within you."

~ Śri Annamalai Swami [15]

Of the mind, Śri Ramana Maharshi said:

"The mind is a bundle of thoughts. The thoughts arise because there is the thinker. The thinker is the ego." [16]

Michael Langford, author of *The Most Direct Means to Eternal Bliss*, refers to the I-thought or ego as the 'imposter self' as it pretends to be the real you.

In fact, we can say that all mental faculties are nothing but the ego or imposter self. Our real identity is the Pure Awareness 'behind' all thought/mental activity. This is the subject of the following quote from the teachings of Śri Ramana Maharshi.

> *"The mind is nothing other than the 'I'-thought. The mind and the ego are one and the same. The other mental faculties such as the intellect and the memory are only this. Mind [manas], intellect [buddhi], the storehouse of mental tendencies [citta], and ego [ahaṁkāra]; all these are only the one mind itself. This is like different names being given to a man according to his different functions."* [17]

In the quote given above, the various functions of the mind are listed. Together, these form what Vedānta refers to as the Antaḥkaraṇa or inner instrument.

It may be helpful to highlight here that the Vedāntic definition of citta is different to the one given by yoga. In Vedānta, citta refers to the subconscious mind consisting of submerged experiences and memories.

In yoga, however, citta refers to the mind-stuff or mental substance. It is equivalent to Vedānta's Antaḥkaraṇa. A traditional analogy given in yoga is that the citta is like a lake and thoughts (vṛttis) are likened to the waves or ripples forming upon the surface of the lake. The vṛttis arising in the 'lake' of the mind are of the: manas [mind], buddhi [intellect], and ahaṁkāra (ego). Patañjali categorizes the vṛttis according to their content in yoga sūtra 1.6. These are: pramāṇa (right knowledge/correct perception); viparyaya (wrong knowledge/incorrect perception); vikalpa (imagination/day-dreaming); nidrā (sleep); and smṛti (memory).

EXERCISE 3: **Enquiry into the Ego (I-Thought)**

Consider the quote by Śri Ramana Maharshi presented at the beginning of this chapter:

"The 'I' thought is said to be the sum total of all thoughts. The source of the 'I' thought has to be enquired into."

Take time to deeply contemplate on the following and relate it to your own everyday experience:

All thought is transient. Every thought that you have arises and disappears in your awareness, which is the Self.

The source of all thought, including the I-thought (ego), is the Self because the Self is there first. It is the awareness in which the I-thought, or indeed any thought, appears to arise.

CHAPTER 4

Self-Enquiry by Subject-Object Discrimination

"You are not the physical body, nor the vital force (Prāṇa), nor the sense organs, nor the mind, nor the intellect, nor the ego. You are not any of these, either individually or collectively. That supreme witness-ing consciousness, that pure resplendent Being, you are That."
~ Ādi Śaṅkarācārya[18]

IN THIS chapter we will enquire into the nature of experience. If you reflect for a moment, you will observe that your entire waking life consists of a stream of successive experiences: you see, hear,

> *"If you wish to be free,*
> *Know you are the Self.*
> *The Witness of all these,*
> *The heart of awareness."*
>
> ~ Aṣṭāvakra Gītā [19]

taste, touch, smell, think, desire etc. All of this arises in your mind. Using sound as an example, a simplified description of hearing a telephone ring is as follows:

> The sound waves created by the phone enter the outer ear and travel through the ear canal to the ear drum. This causes the eardrum to vibrate, sending an electrical signal via the auditory nerve to the brain. The brain converts that signal into a sound. All of this is mind activity (vṛtti or mental modification) enabling us to recognize sound.

We can affirm that, as the phone rings, the sound it makes is an object of our awareness.

A similar analysis can be applied to the sensory experiences of sight, taste, touch and smell. All are experienced as thought or mental modification (vṛtti). On reflection one observes that the awareness or witness of all these is the same.

Every experience, without exception, has two components: our awareness and an object of perception (mental modification).

This is the subject of the following verse in Pañcadaśī:

"The objects of sense knowledge (sound, sight, touch and smell) that are perceived in the waking state have different properties but the Awareness of these is one." ~ Verse I.3

Let us now proceed to Exercise 4. Read the instructions one or two times and then begin. The suggested duration is ten minutes or more.

EXERCISE 4:
Self-Enquiry by Subject-Object Discrimination

- Look out at the room (your external environment).
- Notice your awareness looking out through your eyes at the room.
- Close your eyes and notice that your awareness is still there.
- With the eyes remaining closed, observe external sounds as they come and go in your awareness. Notice that the awareness remains when a particular sound is no longer heard.
- As a thought arises in your mind, be aware and witness it. Notice that all your thoughts come and go in the same awareness.

The purpose of the above exercise is for you to begin to become established in your identity as the Ātman or Witness (Sākṣī) — the ultimate subject.

This represents the beginning of a fundamental and crucial shift in identity:

You are not a body plus mind/intellect with a consciousness (awareness). Rather, you are that very consciousness by which all objects of sense perception are revealed.

You, the Pure Consciousness (Ātman), remain completely unaffected by the thoughts or emotions that endlessly come and go.

Objects include your own body and mind/intellect in addition to any external object in the physical universe registered by your five senses. Every object is experienced as a vṛtti (mental modification) illumined by the Ātman.

> *"You cannot see That which is the Seer of seeing; you cannot hear That which is the Hearer of hearing; you cannot think of That which is the Thinker of thought; you cannot know That which is the Knower of knowledge. This is your Self, that is within all; everything else but This is perishable."*
>
> ~ Bṛhadāraṇyaka Upaniṣad
> (Verse III.iv.2)

The Kaṭha Upaniṣad says:

"The sun does not shine there, nor the moon and the stars, nor these lightnings — not to speak of this fire. He shining, everything shines after Him. By his light all this is lighted."*
~ Verse II.ii.15

*In the innermost Self or Ātman which is Pure Awareness.

With this shift in identity there also begins to arise an experiential understanding of why the Self is of the nature 'Existence-Consciousness-Bliss' (Sat-Cit-Ānanda). Swami Tejomayananda, of the Chinmaya Mission explains:

"The Self illumines all our experiences through the years and is itself self-effulgent, hence the nature of Pure Consciousness or Awareness (Cit Svarūpa). It exists eternally, unchanging through ages and is therefore of the nature of pure Existence (Sat Svarūpa). It is loved by all the most, hence it is the source of utmost Bliss (Ānanda Svarūpa). We can conclude through logic (yukti) and our experience (anubhūti) what the Scriptures*

(śruti) declare that the Self is Existence-Consciousness-Bliss (Saccidānanda Svarūpa)." [20]

*That the Self is of the nature of Bliss is demonstrated by one's love for the Self which manifests in the wish 'may I never cease to exist'. From this we can conclude that the Self is the ultimate source of happiness.

Pause for Reflection

Reflect on how the Ātman is constantly Self-revealing in every experience.

When any object (internal* or external) is perceived, whether it be thought, sight, sound, taste, touch, smell, one can investigate (turn one's attention to) that which is aware (the Silent Witness) of the thought, sight, sound, etc.

*"Internal" refers to a mental object, i.e. thought, memory, mental picture, emotion, desire, etc.

CHAPTER 5

Self-Enquiry —
Abiding in the Silence of the Self

"To know the truth of one's Self as the sole Reality, and to merge and become one with it, is the only true Realization. Just be the Self, that is all." ~ Śri Ramana Maharshi

To ABIDE in the Self is simply to focus one's attention solely on the Self within. This is the correct practice of Self-enquiry, as clearly stated by Śri Ramana Maharshi in the following quote*:

> *"Whatever thoughts arise — the mind should not be allowed to go in their direction but should be made to rest in one's self which is the Ātman."*

> **"By the practice of enquiry, the knowledge of Brahman arises; then it cannot be prevented whether one likes it or not. Such knowledge, by the mere fact of its arising, destroys all ideas of the reality of the world."**
>
> ~ Pañcadaśī (Verse IX.75)

*From *Self-Enquiry of Bhagavan Śri Ramana Maharshi* published by Sri Ramanasramam.

Śri Muruganar, a Self-realized disciple of Śri Ramana Maharshi, explains:

> *"Is it not because you are knowledge [i.e. consciousness] itself that you are able to know the world? If [instead of knowing the world] you turn your attention, **taking that***

Consciousness alone as your target, *It will Itself as the Guru reveal the Truth [i.e. Reality]"* ~ Guru Vachaka Kovai*, Saying 432

*Guru Vachaka Kovai (The Garland of Guru's Sayings) by Śri Muruganar is inspired by the teachings of Śri Ramana Maharshi.

Remember! The Self is not a thought construct, and therefore cannot be perceived of as an object. It is the ultimate subject we enquired into in the previous chapter.

The following quote by Michael Langford helps to clarify:

*"The spiritual meaning of the term 'Self-enquiry' is directly looking into one's Self, which can also be described as **Self-attention**. Since the true Self is awareness, this can also be described as attention to Awareness or Awareness aware of itself. This is not two awarenesses watching the other. This is just one Awareness aware of itself. And what is itself? Itself is Awareness. Thus, **Awareness of Awareness**. Directly looking into one's Self is directly looking into Awareness because the Self is Awareness."* [21]

It is only through practicing this method that you will succeed, as the teacher is no other than the Self. Related to this, Śri Nisargadatta Maharaj explained:

"Your own Self is your ultimate teacher. The outer teacher is merely a milestone. It is only your inner teacher that will walk with you to the goal, for he is the goal." [22]

EXERCISE 5: **Abiding in the Silence of the Self**

The suggested duration for this exercise is a minimum of thirty minutes.

Sit in a comfortable position (for example on a chair or sitting cross-legged) and close your eyes. Allow yourself to relax completely, both physically and mentally.

Turn your attention inward away from the world, body and

mind (all mental activity) and towards your awareness.

Watch only your awareness.

If thoughts come, do not try and complete them, just turn your attention back to your awareness watching awareness.

The following are various quotes by Śri Nisargadatta Maharaj, from the book I AM THAT, related to the method for abiding in the Self (described above).

"Giving attention to attention, aware of being aware. Affectionate awareness is the crucial factor that brings Reality into focus."

"Awareness is undivided; awareness is aware of itself."

"When this awareness turns upon itself, you call it the Supreme state."

"What you need is to be aware of being aware."

"Be aware of being conscious and seek the source of consciousness."

"Awareness is unattached and unshaken. It is lucid, silent, peaceful, alert and unafraid, without desire and fear, meditate on it as your true being."

"The seer becomes conscious of himself as the seer."

Abiding in the Self, which may also be referred to as meditation on the Self or being attentive to the I AM, is the only true direct path to Self-realization.

Śri Nisargadatta Maharaj said simply:

"Look at yourself steadily — it is enough." [23]

> **"When the five organs of perception become still, together with the mind, and the intellect ceases to be active: that is called the Supreme State [Brahman]."**
>
> ~ Katha Upanishad
> (Verse II.ii.15)

Do not be disheartened if you find yourself struggling with this practice when you first begin. Consistent daily effort is the key to progress. The process of Self-enquiry is a subtle one, requiring both a calm and discriminating mind. To help purify the mind (make it calm), Patañjali systematized the eight limbs of yoga, the subject of Part 2. To preview, the eight limbs of yoga are: (i) Yamas (moral restraints); (ii) Niyamas (inner observances); (iii) Āsanas (seat or posture); (iv) Prāṇāyāma (control of vital energy); (v) Pratyāhāra (withdrawal of the senses); (vi) Dhāraṇā (concentration); (vii) Dhyāna (meditation); and (viii) Samādhi (deep absorption).

In the beginning, it is necessary to practice this method alone, away from daily activities. This may be a room in your apartment or house where you live, but it must be somewhere that you will not be disturbed. On the need for this, Śri Ramakrishna* explained:

> *"To fix the mind on God is very difficult, in the beginning, unless one practices meditation in solitude. When a tree is young it should be fenced all around; otherwise it may be destroyed by cattle."*
>
> *"If you enter the world without first cultivating love for God, you will be entangled more and more. You will be overwhelmed with its danger, its grief, its sorrows. And the more you think of worldly things, the more you will be attached to them."*
>
> *"First rub your hands with oil and then break open the jack-fruit; otherwise they will be smeared with its sticky milk. First secure the oil of divine love, and then set your hands to the duties of the world."*
>
> ~ The Gospel of Śri Ramakrishna

*Śri Ramakrishna (1836-1886) was an Indian saint. His main disciple, Swami Vivekananda founded the Ramakrishna Math, headquartered in Bellur, India.

While Patañjali's system of yoga helps us develop the necessary mental preparedness for Self-realization, Advaita Vedānta provides us with a framework of understanding that satisfies the intellect. This framework, the subject of the remainder of Part 1, is based on a rational analysis of our experience that we can directly relate to. In his lectures, Swami Vivekananda often highlighted the importance of having intellectual faith as opposed to blind belief.

In Part 2 (in the second limb of yoga or Niyamas) there is one final Self-enquiry exercise which is the analysis of the three states (waking, dreaming and deep sleep) based on Śri Gaudapāda's Māṇḍūkya Kārikā.

CHAPTER 6

Discrimination Between the Permanent and the Transient

"Ātman (the Seer) in itself is alone permanent, the seen is opposed to it (i.e. transient) – such a settled conviction is truly known as discrimination." ~ Aparokṣānubhūti (Verse 5)

"Let nothing disturb you. Let nothing frighten you. Everything passes away except God." ~ Saint Teresa of Avila

Through deep reflection, you may arrive at the direct intuitive understanding that the Seer (Ātman) alone is permanent — the constant, unchanging background of awareness that is never not there.

In contrast, all the possible objects of one's awareness (the 'Seen'), derived from matter or energy, are transient and constantly changing. Nothing in the physical universe lasts in its current form forever.

> *"In as much as all this world, body and organs, vital breath and personality are all unreal, in so much THOU ART THAT, the restful, the stainless, secondless Eternal, the supreme."*
>
> ~ Ādi Śaṅkarācārya [24]

All objects in the physical universe, including the body, are constituted from primordial matter (prakṛti). Prakṛti is composed of the three guṇas (innate qualities) in continuously changing proportions. The three guṇas are: (i) rajas (action); (ii) tamas (inertia); and (iii) sattva (lucidity). You will discover in Chapter 8 that even thoughts (mind/intellect) are made up of matter, albeit in subtle form.

Being able to recognize that everything except the Self (Seer) is subject to change constitutes significant spiritual progress.

> *"Some assert, 'This world before our eyes lacks permanence, 'tis true. But it is real while it lasts. We deny it saying, 'Permanence is a criterion of Reality.'"*
>
> ~ Śri Ramana Maharshi[25]

There is, however, another level of discrimination, distinguishing between the real (Sat) and the unreal (Mithyā). The Sanskrit term 'Sat' refers to the eternal and unchanging Reality, which is of the nature of Pure Consciousness or Pure Awareness. Mithyā means what is false — or only apparently real, absent the knowledge of reality. Once that knowledge dawns, what was once thought to be real is now known to be false.

The following statement represents the next important leap in our understanding:

Only that which is permanent, the Seer (Ātman), is real (Sat). Matter/energy is inert, transient, and ultimately unreal (mithyā).

Thus, we are told in Tattva-Bodha, a text attributed to Ādi Śaṅkarācārya:

> *"What is discrimination? **The Eternal alone is the Reality, apart from it all else is ephemeral, this alone is discrimination.**"* ~ Verse 1.1

Reality (the Seer) alone is eternal, whereas all objects seen and experienced in the physical universe (the Seen) are an appearance only, rather like a mirage. A traditional analogy given in Vedānta is that of a dream. This is the subject of the following verse in Ādi Śaṅkarācārya's Ātma-bodha:

"The world is truly like a dream only: full of its attachments and aversions, and so on. While the dream continues, it appears to be real; when we awaken, its unreality is seen."
~ Verse 6

The process of discrimination between the real (Sat) and the unreal (Mithyā) is an essential step in Self-enquiry — because it is the erroneous belief that we are a limited, separate body that reinforces our ignorance of our real nature. This error keeps us firmly entrenched in saṃsāra, the cycle of birth and death. Yoga sūtra 2.5 tells us:

> *"Whatever takes form is false. Only the formless endures. When you understand The truth of this teaching, You will not be born again."*
>
> ~ Aṣṭāvakra Gītā [26]

"Mistaking the transient for the permanent, the impure for the pure, pain for pleasure, and that which is not the Self [Seen] for the Self [Seer]: all this is called lack of spiritual knowledge, avidyā". [27]

It is the continuous practice of discrimination (viveka) between the real and the unreal that destroys spiritual ignorance; and along with it, all suffering. This is the subject of yoga sūtra 2.26:

*"The ceaseless flow of **discriminative knowledge** in thought, word and deed destroys ignorance, the source of pain".* [28]

You may feel strong resistance to statements regarding the unreality of the world that is seen everyday. Please bear with me! In the forthcoming chapters we will be putting this in the context of our spiritual practice. And in Part 2, it will hopefully become clear why, for Self-realization, we must have the firm conviction that the world is an appearance, and that the Self alone is the permanent Reality. This is also emphasized by Śri Vāsiṣṭha in the following quote*:

"Neither freedom from sorrow nor realization of one's real nature is possible as long as the conviction does not arise in one that the world-appearance is unreal." [29]

*From the classic text Yoga Vāsiṣṭha.

The point is not to deny your experience of the world. Having said that, your experience of the world does not make it Reality. Neither does its appearance equal actual Existence.

Ātman, your real nature, is devoid of objects. It is empty as it contains "no-thing". It is, however, full of itself, its very nature being Absolute Existence (Sat), Absolute Consciousness (Cit) and Absolute Bliss (Ānanda).

Pause for Reflection

Let us pause for a moment to reflect on the aim of Self-enquiry and how it relates to these pages.

Our aim is to remove ignorance (avidyā) which may be defined as both:

- taking the body (plus mind/intellect) to be the Self; and
- perceiving the world of external objects to be real (Sat).

Ignorance can be removed only by knowledge — knowledge of what we truly are. And through Self-enquiry, you are hopefully beginning to discriminate your true essence from the not-Self. It is only once we intuit the Self that we can rest or abide in our true nature — the focus of Chapter 5.

In this chapter, I have attempted to demonstrate through rational analysis, that the impermanent external world of names and objects is only apparently real (mithyā). The deeper purpose of which will be uncovered in the next chapter.

CHAPTER 7

Negation of the False ('Neti, Neti')

*"When the apparent reality of the world is removed,
all that remains is pure Being". ~ Ādi Śaṅkarācārya[30]*

*"And when he was demanded of the Pharisees, when the
kingdom of God should come, he answered them and said,
The kingdom of God cometh not with observation:
Neither shall they say, Lo here! or, lo there! for, behold,
the kingdom of God is within you." ~ Luke 17:20-21*

WHEN we carry out Self-enquiry, it must be from one's own perspective in order to develop intuitive understanding. This is the purpose behind the sequential series of Self-enquiry exercises given in the preceding chapters.

> *"The entire world (severally and collectively) that can be referred to as 'this' can be negated, but the thing which is not 'this' can never be negated and this indestructible witness is the Self ."*
>
> ~ Pañcadaśī (Verse III.33)

You are now grounding yourself in the understanding that your real nature is Pure Consciousness (or Pure Awareness), even though you have the illusory experience of being a separate individual.

When we negate all that is false or only apparently real (mithyā), which includes the body and mind and the entire physical world, we are left with the truth. The name we give to this truth is Brahman.

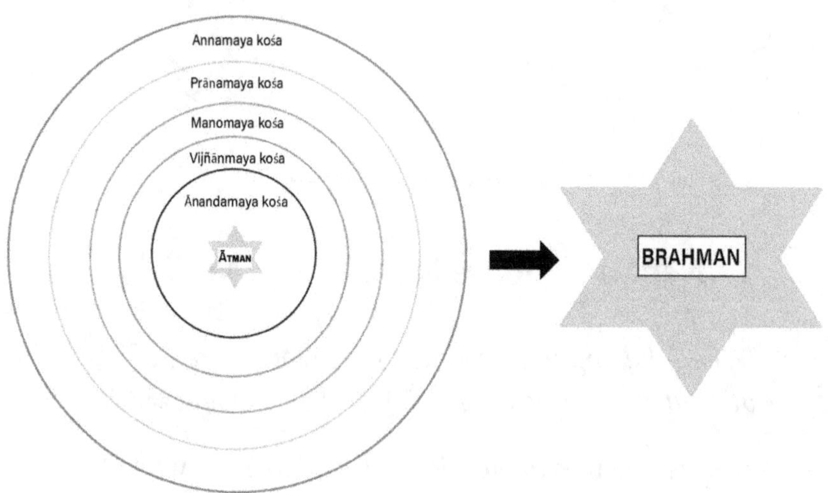

Hence, we learn what Brahman is by negating all that it is not. In Sanskrit this process is called "Neti, Neti" which means "Not this, Not this" and is the subject of the following verse from the Bṛhadāraṇyaka Upaniṣad:

> *"Now therefore the description (of Brahman): 'Not this, not this'. Because there is no other and more appropriate description than this 'Not this'. Now Its name: 'The Truth of truth'. The vital force is truth, and It is the Truth of that".* ~ Verse II.iii.6

> **"The Reality (Truth) is One: the wise call it by various names."**
>
> ~ Ṛgveda (Verse 1.164.46)

The word Ātman is mainly used from the individual's standpoint — one's inner Self. It should be noted, however, that the words Ātman and Brahman are often used interchangeably as they are pointing to the same Pure Consciousness that you are. In his commentary to Ātma-bodha, Swami Nikhilananda* explains:

> *"Ātman is the deathless, birthless, eternal, and real substance in every individual. It is the unchanging Reality behind the changing body, sense-organs, mind, and ego. It is Spirit, which*

is Pure Consciousness and is unaffected by time, space, and causality; therefore It is limitless and One without a second. As the unchanging Reality in the individual is called Ātman, so the unchanging Reality in the universe is called Brahman. Brahman, too, is beyond time, space, and causality and is all-pervading Spirit. Vedānta states that Brahman and Ātman are one and the same. The knowledge of this identity or non-difference is called Self-Knowledge, which confers upon a man the boon of liberation from the bondage and suffering of the world." [31]

*Swami Nikhilananda (1895 to 1973) was a direct disciple of Śri Sarada Devi, the wife of Śri Ramakrishna. His most important works include translations (with commentaries) of the Upaniṣads, the Bhagavad Gītā and other Vedāntic works.

> **"There the eye goes not, speech goes not, nor the mind. We know not, we understand not, how would one teach it?**
>
> **Other is it indeed than the known, and moreover above the unknown. Thus from the forbearers, the doctrine has been transmitted to us."**
>
> ~ Kena Upaniṣad (Verses I.3, I.4)

Pause for Reflection

The process of negation (neti, neti) which naturally follows on from our discrimination between the permanent and the transient (the subject of the previous chapter), reveals the profound truth that the same ONE inner essence (Pure Consciousness or Pure Awareness) at the core of each and every one of us, is the underlying substratum of the entire world of external objects (names and forms).

It is worth spending a few moments to reflect on this.

Chapter 8

How the Impossible Appeared to Happen

"It is useless to search for the teeth of a crow, for it has no teeth.
Similar is the case with the son of a barren woman, a lotus grown in
the sky, a city in the clouds, and the horns of a hare. This is to show
that it is meaningless to question about the contradictions and
mysteries of existence like "Why did the Perfect God create an
imperfect world?" etc., for there is no real change and there
is no creation at all in reality, and that these questions arise
so long as the Sun of wisdom has not arisen".
~ Swami Sivananda

"Before the mountains were born
or you brought forth the whole world,
from everlasting to everlasting you are God."
~ Psalm 90:2

IN THE previous chapter, by the process of 'Neti Neti' or negation of the false (mithyā), we arrived at the understanding that:
The Self or Ātman (one's true identity) is Brahman.

There are not two entities called Ātman and Brahman, they are one and the same. And this is what you are!

We have now worked our way to the ultimate truth, expressed succinctly by Ādi Śaṅkarācārya:

"Brahman alone is real. The world is an appearance.
The individual is no other than Brahman"
~ Brahmajñānāvalīmālā (Verse 20)

Advaita means 'not two' or without a second. In the world, however, we experience duality: our self (subject) experiences a multitude of external objects. After negating all that is false, there are no objects or second "thing" to be aware of. Only Brahman is. This is non-duality.

Questions will naturally arise: "How did the appearance of the world occur?" and "Why are we having the experience of individuality?"

Now we need to consider what Advaita Vedānta refers to as three levels of 'reality' or truth. These are listed as follows, along with the Sanskrit terms:

- Brahman, the Absolute and Sole Reality (Pāramārthika)
- Perceived reality – the material universe of names & forms/multiplicity (Vyāvahārika). Also referred to as relative, transactional, or empirical reality.
- Subjective reality such as the dream state (Prātibhāsika).

However, Brahman and the perceived universe of names and forms are not two independent realities. There is only one Reality and that is Brahman.

In the same way that we know a dream (prātibhāsika) to be false upon waking, the world appearance (vyāvahārika) is also false or illusory from the standpoint of Absolute Reality or Brahman (pāramārthika).

Hence Self-realization may be described as an awakening from the dream of separation. But there is still the great paradox: Brahman, being Perfect Oneness, 'knows' nothing of this world of plurality, because how can there be anything outside of Perfect Oneness? And yet right now, our experience is one of duality.

To get around this paradox and offer an explanation, we must consider the Absolute Reality (pāramārthika) and relative reality (vyāvahārika) as two mutually exclusive standpoints:

Pāramārthika Standpoint: Brahman, the Absolute and Sole Reality

The only true Existence is non-dual Pure Consciousness, also referred to as Nirguṇa Brahman (without attributes) or Para Brahman — the 'Highest' Brahman above all descriptions. From this non-dual standpoint, there is no world. Nor is there any appearance of a world.

Lord Krishna tells us in the Bhagavad Gītā:

"The unreal never is; the Real never is not. This truth indeed has been seen by those who can see the true." ~ Verse 2.16

Śri Gaudapāda, traditionally referred to as Ādi Śaṅkarācārya's guru's guru, emphatically denies any creation (or causality) of the empirical world. This is demonstrated by the following two quotes from Śri Gaudapāda's commentary (kārikā) on the Māṇḍūkya Upaniṣad:

"No jiva [individual] ever comes into existence, There exists no cause that can produce it. The Supreme truth is that nothing is ever born." ~ Verse III.48

"The unreal cannot have the unreal as its cause, nor can the real be produced from the unreal. The real cannot be the cause of the real. And it is much more impossible for the real to be the cause of the unreal!" ~ Verse IV.40

The following quotes also describe the pāramārthika standpoint.

*"Is there a greater folly than the aching folly of supposing that the Self, the I of pure awareness **which does not see this changing world at all**, is subject to some change?"*
~ Guru Vachaka Kovai (Verse 905)

"In truth, this world does not arise from the absolute nor does it merge in it. The absolute alone exists now and forever." ~ Yoga-Vāsiṣṭha[32]

*"All this is mere imagination or thought. Even now nothing has ever been created; The pure infinite space **alone** exists."* ~ Yoga-Vāsiṣṭha[33]

Vyāvahārika Standpoint: Level of the Perceived Universe

Some of the quotes in this section use terms such as 'create' and 'creation'. In the text, I have also used the words 'projection' or 'separation' as these terms are more closely aligned with the highest truth that no 'creation' actually takes place.

The following description of 'how the impossible seemed to happen' is based on the Vedāntic model of creation, which has some similarities to the Sāṁkhyan model closely associated with the yoga school of philosophy. The significance of this is discussed in chapter 11.

This description is relatively brief, intended only to provide helpful insight to your yoga sādhanā (spiritual practice).

A cautionary note: It must be remembered that the story of creation is just that, a story. Swami Sivananda explains:

"Nobody knows how this universe came into being. You will find in the Ṛgveda: 'Who knows here, who can here state whence came all this multifarious Universe? Even the Devas [Gods] are posterior to its creation, who then knows whence this came out?' (Ṛgveda VIII-17-6)."[34]

The fact that, from the standpoint of Absolute Reality (Nirguṇa Brahman), there is no world is why any descriptions or metaphors used to explain the process of creation can never be entirely satisfactory. Unresolvable paradoxes will always persist. Nor will you find complete consistency between the various scriptural sources.

[If during the next section you find the level of detail off-putting, I suggest you move forwards to the section headed 'Level of the Jiva (Individual)' on page 57. If you do decide to jump to page 57, you will still get to read a high-level summary of this chapter, in addition to an outline of its practical relevance. You can always visit this chapter again later to read it in its entirety if you wish.]

How the Impossible Seemed to Happen

In Brahman, or Perfect Oneness, the impossible seemed to occur. There arose a thought of separation: the idea to create. For example, in the Aitareya Upaniṣad it is said:

"In the beginning this world was the Self (Ātman), one alone, and there was no other being at all that blinked an eye. He thought to himself: Let me create the worlds." ~ Verse I.i.1

How is it possible for thought to arise in perfect Oneness? For want of a better explanation, the answer Vedānta gives is Māyā: the illusory, inexplicable power of Brahman. In the Brahma Sūtras it is explained:

"Brahman is pure Intelligence itself, Unchangeable. All-knowingness and creation are not possible for Brahman.
To this objection it can be replied that Brahman can be All-knowing and creative through His illusory power, Māyā."[35]

Why would Brahman wish to create? An answer sometimes given is 'Līlā', the divine play or sport of Brahman.

A second, perhaps better response is that there is no answer! The question itself is illogical as Brahman never created anything or changed in any way. From the Pāramārthika Standpoint (Brahman — the Absolute and Sole Reality), there is no Māyā.

Back to the Vyāvahārika Standpoint (level of the perceived universe):

The very instant the thought of separation appeared to enter, there was a forgetting of Reality (ajñāna).

Māyā's powers are both projecting and veiling. The result of Māyā's veiling power has already been described as the forgetting of Reality (ajñāna) which appears to occur with the first thought of separation. Now, Māyā is free to use her projecting power. The first entity to evolve is the Cosmic Mind (Hiraṇyagarbha).

Swami Nikhilananda, in his commentary on the Kaṭha Upaniṣad, describes the first manifestation:

"The first manifestation of Pure Brahman, due to Its association with ajñāna, is called the Unmanifest. This latter may be compared to a seed just before the coming forth of the sprout. The first entity to emerge from the Unmanifest is Hiraṇyagarbha, also known by such other epithets as Brahmā (the World Soul, or the Cosmic Mind) and Prāna (the Cosmic Life)." [36]

Māyā's two powers are the subject of the following quote:

"Two powers, undoubtedly, are predicated of Māyā, viz., those of projecting and veiling. The projecting power creates everything from the subtle body to the gross universe."
~ Dṛg-Dṛśya-Viveka (Verse 13)

However, the projection of the world through Māyā is not something different or apart from Brahman, but a seeming transformation of Brahman. It is Brahman alone that appears to manifest as all these names and forms. The analogy given in Dṛg-Dṛśya-Viveka is that of foam or waves upon the ocean, which we know to consist of water alone.

*"The manifesting of all names and forms in the entity which is Existence-Consciousness-Bliss and **which is the same as Brahman**, like the foam etc. in the ocean, is known as creation."* ~ Dṛg-Dṛśya-Viveka (Verse 14)

With this in mind, we will now look at the effects of Māyā's projecting power in a little more detail. But before we do, we must first examine the causal or unmanifest state.

Causal (Unmanifest) State

The preliminary stage of creation is the 'birth' of prakṛti (primordial matter), composed of the three guṇas (rajas, tamas and sattva). Prakṛti is the disturbance in Brahman that occurs simultaneously with the first thought of separation. Now Brahman, in association with Māyā, is referred to as Saguṇa Brahman or Īśvara, the Creator God.

The three guṇas are the building blocks that Māyā uses for her projection. Everything that has name and form in the empirical universe is composed of them. This is described in the following quote from Ādi Śaṅkarācārya's Tattva Bodha.

"Depending on Brahman; being of the nature of Sattva, Rajas and Tamas, the 3 qualities of Nature, Māyā exists." ~ Tattva Bodha (Verse 11.1)

The Unmanifest or Causal state is the apex of creation. Nothing has yet been created or projected but exists as potential only. In the following quote, Swami Sivananda uses the metaphor of a seed to describe the relationship between the unmanifest and manifest:

"In summer the whole earth is parched. As soon as there is a shower the seeds sprout and plants come out. They were in an unmanifested state before the rains. Even so the world which is in a manifested state had an unmanifested state. It has come out of Māyā, the Causal body of Īśvara."* [37]

*Īśvara arises, as it were, on account of Māyā. Māyā, therefore, is said to be the causal body of Īśvara.

From the unmanifest state evolves the subtle and gross (physical) creation. We will now see how Īśvara (Saguṇa Brahman)

— the cosmic causal body, transforms itself into the physical universe.

Subtle Creation

First Saguṇa Brahman gives rise to the five subtle elements (tanmātras), each composed of the three guṇas. They are referred to as subtle because they cannot be perceived by the senses. The five subtle elements evolve in the following order: space or ether (ākāśa), air (vāyu), fire (agni), water (jal) and earth (prithvi).

As emphasized earlier, nothing independent or apart from Brahman is being created. This applies equally to both the subtle and gross creation. This is further clarified by Swami Nikhilananda:

> *"The first element to evolve from Saguṇa Brahman is ākāśa, which is usually translated as 'space' or 'sky,' and sometimes as 'ether.' The creation, or evolution, of ākāśa really means that Brahman, in association with māyā, appears as ākāśa. From ākāśa evolves air (vāyu); that is to say, Brahman, in association with māyā, appearing as ākāśa, further appears as air."* [38]

The sattvic portion of the subtle elements is utilized to create the mind, intellect, and five organs of knowledge (jñānendriyas). The jñānendriyas are the following subtle faculties of knowledge: hearing, touch, sight, taste and smell. The rajasic portion is used to create the five Prāṇas and the five organs of action (karmendriyas). The karmendriyas are the following subtle faculties of action: speech, hands, feet, the organs of excretion and procreation.

Each subtle body thus consists of seventeen components: five organs of knowledge; five organs of action; five Prāṇas; the mind; and the intellect.

Hiraṇyagarbha or the 'Cosmic Mind' is the sum total of all the subtle bodies.

Gross (Physical) Creation

From the tamasic portion of the subtle elements evolve the five gross or physical elements (Mahā Bhūtas) — space, air, fire, water and earth in physical (perceivable) form. Each gross element contains one half portion of its subtle counterpart plus one eighth of each of the other four subtle elements.

The five gross elements are the building blocks that make up the physical universe. From Hiraṇyagarbha (cosmic mind), through the power of Māyā, the entire physical universe of multiplicity is projected, and with it, time and space.

Virāṭ is the name given to the sum total of all the physical bodies or the entire physical manifestation of living and non-living objects.

Level of the Jiva (Individual)

The Causal, Subtle and Gross (Physical) stages of creation have been described above at the cosmic level.

At the level of the individual or jiva, the causal body (kāraṇa śarīra), which originates with ignorance (avidyā) of one's real nature, is the cause or seed of the subtle body (sūkṣma śarīra) and gross body (sthūla śarīra).

The causal body is the seat of our vāsanās (innate tendencies) which determine every aspect of our birth including the nature or characteristics of our mind (intellect and thoughts, etc) and physical body.

The jiva (individual) becomes fully embodied by all three bodies, all of which are external to the Ātman (Self). As there is an infinite combination of sattva, rajas and tamas, so is there an infinite variety of beings. Our experience is that we are a separate body and mind, one of many, living in a world external to us.

Ignorance (avidyā) is at the root of all our problems as we now falsely identify ourselves to be a separate body, vulnerable to lack, attack, sickness, and finally death.

Hence, avidyā is the first affliction (Kleśa) listed in yoga sūtra 2.3, and the root cause of the other four afflictions(s): asmitā (individuality/ego); rāga (intense likes, attachments); dveṣa (dislikes, special hates); and abhiniveśa (clinging to life, fear of death).

Our likes and dislikes (including all attachments) comprise all our desires. The nature of our desires is governed by the constantly changing proportions of the three guṇas (rajas, tamas and sattva).

Swami Krishnananda in his commentary on Swami Sivananda's book The Moksha Gita refers to the degeneration of consciousness that seemingly occurs on separation from Brahman:

"It first forgets the reality; secondly it centers its consciousness in a localized body; thirdly it drags other external bodies to itself and regards such of the few as are beneficial to its egoistic pleasures as its own self and consequently begins to hate those entities or individuals which are not connected with its interests or are set in opposition to it." [39]

But in the Kaṭha Upaniṣad it is also said:

"The self–existent Supreme Lord inflicted an injury upon the sense–organs in creating them with outgoing tendencies; therefore a man perceives only outer objects with them and not the inner Self. But a calm person, wishing for Immortality, beholds the inner Self with his eyes closed." ~ Verse II.i.1

Ignorance (avidyā), in addition to karma or the law of cause and effect, is beginningless*. And yet, for all of us, ignorance must come to an end as our very nature is divine. Swami Nikhilananda in his commentary to Ātma Bodha explains:

"Māyā is without beginning; that is to say, a man under the spell of māyā cannot know its beginning, just as a sleeper, while experiencing a dream, cannot know its beginning."
"..the very concepts of time, space, and causality, the pillars of the relative world, belong to māyā." [40]

*Hindu cosmology upholds an infinite cycle of universes. Eventually, the current universe will be destroyed after which remains the causal (unmanifest or potential) state prior to the next creation-maintenance-destruction cycle.

Brahman: The Intelligent and Material Cause

As described above, the supreme cause of the world is the first thought of separation that appears to arise in Perfect Oneness ("He thought to himself: 'Let me create the worlds'"). Hence, Brahman is the efficient or intelligent cause of the universe (Nimitta-Kāraṇa).

> *"Just as the spider stretches forth and gathers together its threads, as herbs grow out of the earth, as from a living man comes out the hair, so also from the imperishable comes out this universe."*
>
> ~ Muṇḍaka Upaniṣad (Verse I.i.7)

As there is no thought in the non-dual Brahman, this is said to come only after Brahman appears to accept the limitation of Māyā. Brahman is then referred to as Saguṇa Brahman or Īśvara.

This perspective is further explained by Swami Nikhilananda in the following quote.

"In the beginning — that is to say, before the evolution of names and forms, time and space — Ātman, or Brahman, alone exists. Then It becomes conditioned by Māyā, Its own inscrutable power. At that time Brahman is called Saguṇa Brahman–Mahesvara, or the Great Lord. The idea of creation arises in His mind. Sa aikshata — 'He thought.' Then Brahman, on account of māyā, forgets, as it were,

*Its infinite nature and regards Itself as an individual
entity. It says: 'I am one; I shall be many.'"* [41]

The following quote from The Brahma Sūtras explains why
Saguṇa Brahman is to be understood as the intelligent cause of
the world.

*"Creation of ākāśa, fire, wind, water is done solely to God's
will. One element cannot create another element out of its
own power. It is God in the form of one element that creates
another element there-from by His will. The elements are
inert. They have no power to create. Brahman Himself acting
from within the elements was the real creator of all those
elements."* [42]

Saguṇa Brahman is not only the intelligent cause but the
material cause of the world (upādāna-kāraṇa). As described
above, the world appears to arise by way of transformation or
modification. It is primarily for this reason that Saguṇa Brahman is to be understood to be the material cause. The world appearance, in all its stages of manifestation (causal, subtle and
gross), is never actually apart from Brahman.

Hence, we learn from Śrī Vyāsa in his Brahma Sūtras that:

*"The World (effect) is non-different from Brahman (the
Cause)."* [43]

Now to Take Your Understanding Deeper Still

But the description given above of Brahman transforming itself into the physical world (like the ocean becoming waves and
foam) is there only to help us make sense of our experience of
separation in the empirical world (Vyāvahārika level).

The truth is that the Infinite cannot become the finite.

At best, the projection of the world through Māyā can be described only as an apparent transformation, not an actual one.

Swami Sivananda further clarifies:

"According to Śri Śaṅkara, there is one Absolute Brahman who is Sat-ānanda, who is of an absolutely homogenous nature. The appearance of this world is due to Māyā — the illusory power of Brahman which is neither Sat or Asat. This world is unreal. This world is a Vivarta or **apparent modification** through Māyā. Brahman appears as this universe through Māyā. Brahman is the only reality."* [44]

*Sat refers to the unchanging permanent Reality. Asat is opposite — that which is changing and impermanent.

If the world is only an apparent modification through Māyā, it must be an appearance only – an appearance superimposed upon Brahman. Swami Sivananda explains the fundamental Vedāntic principle of superimposition (Adhyāropa) in the following quote.

> *"Adhyāropa is the result of ignorance of the real object. Generally, people mistake a rope for a snake, a post for a man, the mother-of-pearl for silver, the mirage for water, etc.*
>
> *In hazy light of dusk you mistake a rope to be a snake. You are terribly afraid of it. But a friend of yours who comes with a light assures you that it is only a rope. Now you look at the supposed snake once again and find it to be unmoving and that it is really a rope and not a snake. Now the Adhyāropa vanishes. In this instance there was no snake at all. It was only the rope that appeared as a snake. The snake was not there in the past, is not in the present and will not be there in the future (three periods of time), i.e. neither before you saw the snake, nor when you were actually seeing the snake, nor, again after your friend came with the light and assured you it was only a rope, was there really a snake."* [45]

Superimposition occurs due to not knowing (or ignorance of) the real object. Also, superimposition is dependent on there being an underlying real object. In the examples given in the quote above, the real object is the: rope (not snake), post (not man), etc.

Similarly, the appearance of the world depends on Nirguṇa Brahman, the substratum of Reality which is Pure Consciousness.

Back to the Highest Truth

But even this perspective, that the world is an appearance superimposed on Brahman, is given to help explain our experience at the Vyāvahārika standpoint (empirical world).

At the Pāramārthika Standpoint (Nirguṇa Brahman), there is neither creation (by transformation) nor appearance (through superimposition) of a world. Śri Ramana Maharshi reminds us:

> *"What is Self's self-transformation as the world?*
> *A twist of straw appearing as a snake?*
> *Look hard you see no snake at all.*
> *There was no transformation, no creation, no world at all."*
> ~ Guru Vachaka Kovai (Verse 87)

Given that nothing is created* and there is no change whatsoever in the Indivisible Supreme Reality, Brahman is only the fictitious material cause. Similarly, as the Supreme Reality is actionless, Brahman is the apparent efficient/intelligent cause.

*From the perspective of the highest truth.

Pause for Reflection

In this chapter I have described the world from three perspectives:

(i)   A world of multiplicity (names and forms) created by the seeming transformation of Brahman due to its association with Māyā.

(ii)   An appearance of a world of multiplicity superimposed, through Māyā, on Brahman.

(iii)   Pure undifferentiated Consciousness (Pāramārthika Standpoint).

These are depicted in the following three successive verses in the Aṣṭāvakra Gītā which are worth reading slowly to allow time for contemplation.

The first verse describes the unbounded Pure Consciousness transforming itself into the worlds of names and forms using the analogy of waves on the ocean, both of which consist of the same stuff (water); the second verse describes the worlds as an appearance arising in the infinite ocean of Pure Consciousness; and the last verse represents the ultimate non-dual truth.

As you read these verses, please try to do so from the core of your being — your quiet centre.

"I am the unbounded deep,
In whom the waves of all the worlds
Naturally rise and fall.
But I do not rise or fall."

"I am the infinite deep
In whom all the worlds
Appear to rise.
Beyond all form,
Forever still.
Even so am I."

"I am not in the world.
The world is not in me.
I am pure.
I am unbounded." [46]

Before we end this pause for reflection it may also be helpful to consider once again the dream analogy. To the one dreaming, it seems that everything 'seen' in the dream is real and external to the dreamer. And yet we know for a fact that everything dreamt (all the dream objects) consists of nothing but the mind of the dreamer. Śri Ramana Maharshi explains:

> *"Lying down on your bed in a closed room with eyes closed you dream of a city, the crowds there and you among. A certain body is identified as yourself in the dream. The city and the rest could not have entered into the room and into your brain: however, such wide space and duration of time were all perceptible to you. They must have been projected from the brain."* ~ Talks, 177

Similarly, the cosmic mind, through Māyā, projects the world of multiplicity which now appears to exist externally to you, the waker. But all that is perceived in the waking state — including the body, mind, and world, is the one Pure Consciousness (Brahman) alone appearing as all these names and forms. Swami Nikhilananda further clarifies:

> *"The diversity experienced in the waking state, like that perceived in dreams, is the activity of the mind, through māyā. The mind is superimposed through ignorance upon the non-dual Ātman. To the knower of Reality the mind is Brahman*, just as to the knower of the rope the illusory snake is the rope, or to the awakened man the dream experience is nothing but the mind".* [47]

*As described earlier in this chapter (see sub-section 'Subtle Creation'), the mind evolves through the apparent transformation of Brahman due to its association with Māyā. This was later described using the principle of superimposition.

The Secret to Self-Realization

Eventually we must conclude that all questions related to the manifestation or creation of the world can never be satisfactorily answered because the mind itself is a product of Māyā.

It is only upon Self-realization, when we wake up from the dream of separation, that all answers are known — because there are no questions.

Imagine you are having a dream and a figure approaches you to inform you that you are experiencing a dream. Questions like 'why am I having a dream?' or 'when and how did the dream begin?' cannot possibly be answered from within the dream itself. Only by waking up will true knowledge dawn, at which point all questions about the origin of the dream will dissolve along with it.

The fundamental purpose for presenting the creation story, and the various perspectives described above, is to help you develop the understanding that the world you currently perceive as something apart from you is an appearance only. This is emphasized by Swami Sivananda:

> *"The Sruti texts* that deal with creation, such as 'From the Ātman sprang Ākāśa, from Ākāśa Vāyu, from Vāyu Agni,' etc., are only intended for giving preliminary instructions to the neophytes or young aspirants; for they cannot grasp at once the Ajātivāda or the theory of non-evolution**. When you read the passages which talk of creation, always remember that all this is only Adhyāropa or superimposition. Never forget this. **Never think even for a second that the world is real. If the world is real, if duality is real, you cannot have experience of Advaitic Realization".** [48]*

*The Upaniṣads fall into this category.

**Ajātivāda or the doctrine of non-origination is referring to the ultimate truth that there is no creation or change in the Absolute Reality (Nirguṇa Brahman).

The Self — the ongoing Presence or Awareness shining in each seemingly fragmented mind—is there to help you remember what you truly are, which is Pure Consciousness (or Awareness). Then you have the choice to withdraw your belief in the reality of the world, understanding it to be but a miscreated dream.

You are now able to choose again.

By identifying with your Awareness, the ancient memory of what you truly are, you are making the choice of perfect Oneness (Reality) over the dream of separation.*

> *"Time, space, and causation are like the glass through which the Absolute is seen, and when It is seen on the lower side, It appears as the universe. Now we at once gather from this that in the Absolute there is neither time, space, nor causation. The idea of time cannot be there, seeing that there is no mind, no thought. The idea of space cannot be there, seeing that there is no external change. What you call motion and causation cannot exist where there is only One. We have to understand this, and impress it on our minds, that what we call causation begins after, if we may be permitted to say so, the degeneration of the Absolute into the phenomenal, and not before; that our will, our desire and all these things always come after that."*
>
> ~ Swami Vivekananda [49]

Here lies the secret to Self-realization. In his introduction to his commentary on the Kena Upaniṣad, Ādi Śaṅkarācārya states:

> *"By the knowledge of the identity of the inmost Self and Brahman, ajñāna (ignorance), which is the seed of saṃsāra and the cause of desires and of the flow of activity, is entirely destroyed."*

* In Chapter 6, I emphasized that for Self-realization, one must have the firm conviction that the Self alone is the permanent reality. It is by this conviction that one becomes grounded in this choice.

Pause for Reflection

Reflect for a moment on the nature of your mind. Here I use the word 'mind' in the broadest sense.

On examination you will hopefully observe that your mind appears to be split between:

SELF — the background of awareness (witness consciousness); and

Imposter self or ego — thought or the thinking mind.

Notice also that there is a 'decision maker' part of your mind which is a function of the intellect (buddhi). The decision maker represents your free will. At any given moment you can choose to turn your attention to the Self (quiet center) rather than perpetuating a particular train of thought.

Notice too how the Self exists in the eternal present moment (the NOW). In contrast, all our thoughts relate only to the past or to the future, and never to the present.

CHAPTER 9

All This is Brahman

"For God is infinite,
Within the body and without,
Like a mirror,
And the image in a mirror"
~ Aṣṭāvakra Gītā [50]

IN THIS short but important chapter, we will examine the principle of superimposition (Adhyāropa), and how it relates to our spiritual practice (sādhana). I have also included a visualization exercise to help you turn the theory into concrete enquiry.

In the previous chapter I described how, through Māyā's projecting and veiling powers, the world is superimposed on Brahman.

The world, however real or solid it seems to be, is an appearance only. Swami Sivananda tells us:

"In reality, this world was never created. This world is superimposed on Brahman. This world is imagined where there exists only Brahman." [51]

The first step in Self-enquiry, which has been our main focus up until now, is learning to discriminate between the Seer and the Seen; and for you to become established in the knowledge that the real you is Pure Consciousness (Ātman or Brahman).

But there is a second crucial step that must also be incorporated into our sādhana. In order to give up the illusion of being a separate self, limited to a body, we are to:

Behold the One Undivided essence of Saccidānanda [Brahman] in all names and forms.

The term "names and forms" refers to all objects (sentient and non-sentient) in the physical universe.

One's attitude should be: I alone am all this as I am the inner Self of all beings. The names and forms are a false appearance, just like a mirage.

A helpful metaphor is that of a mirror and its image. Although we see an image in the mirror, we know it to be an appearance only. Every bit of what we see is actually the mirror.

So that this does not remain an intellectual concept only, please carry out the following visualization exercise.

VISUALIZATION: **Ocean of Awareness**

This exercise is inspired by the following verse in the Aṣṭāvakra Gītā. Read the verse and instructions once or twice and then proceed.

"Like bubbles in the sea,
All the worlds arise in you.
Know you are the Self.
Know you are one.
Let yourself dissolve."[52]

Close your eyes and draw your attention to your Self. Be in your own presence for a few minutes.

Using the power of your imagination, visualize your awareness slowly expanding outward from your heart center in all directions. Allow it to encompass the entire physical universe: all the planets, stars, and galaxies. An infinite ocean of awareness that knows no boundaries.

Acknowledge that all objects (seen and unseen), including your own body and that of others; the Earth; moon; and stars, all appear to rise and fall in that awareness.* Like bubbles in the sea, they are all impermanent and eventually collapse back into their true nature which is Pure Awareness.

*In Chapter 4, we saw how all objects arise in your mind, i.e. they are presented as a mental construct (vṛtti) to you, the Witness Consciousness.

The purpose of this visualization exercise is for you to begin to assimilate the profound truth that there is no objective universe apart from You, the Pure Awareness. The entire physical universe is nothing but an appearance in Awareness.

This limitless Pure Awareness is Brahman, and it is You! It is also every other being.

Lord Krishna tells us:

"He who sees Me everywhere and sees everything in Me, he never becomes separated from Me, nor do I become separated from him." ~ Bhagavad Gītā (Verse 6.30)

To put into practice the instruction "Behold the One Undivided essence of Saccidānanda in all names and forms" is to 'see' beyond or to 'discard' the names and forms. You will still visibly see the world, yet you will be able to discriminate between the Real (Sat) and the apparently real (mithyā).

Swami Sivananda provides the following guidance:

"When you look at an object behold Brahman which is the one essence and abandon the form as it is illusory and unreal. Have the same attitude towards the other objects which pertain to the other senses." [53]

Therefore, the statement 'All this is Brahman', should not make one think that Brahman is of a non-homogeneous nature. In the Brahma Sūtras, it is explained:

"In Muṇḍaka Upaniṣad II-2-11 we read: 'Brahman indeed is all this.' From this a doubt may arise that Brahman is of a manifold variegated nature, just as in the case of a tree consisting of leaves, branches, stem, root etc. In order to remove this doubt the text declares in the passage under discussion 'Know Him alone as the Self' i.e. know the Self alone and not that which is merely a product of Avidyā (ignorance) and is false or illusory. Another scriptural text reproves the man who thinks that this world is real. 'From death to death goes he who beholds any difference here.' (Kaṭha Upaniṣad II-4-11)." [54]

When we are able to correctly understand and assimilate this teaching, we begin to awaken our true vision, which is not the vision we see with our physical eyes. In the Bhagavad Gītā, Lord Krishna refers to this as same sightedness or equal vision. It is deep insight that "All indeed is Brahman".

Lord Krishna describes one with same sightedness:

"Sages look with an equal eye on a Brahmana endowed with learning and humility, on a cow, on an elephant, and even on a dog and an outcaste." ~ Bhagavad Gītā (Verse 5.18)

When everything, including ourself and those around us, is understood to be Brahman, there is no longer room for hate or fear.

Our spiritual practice then should also focus on how we see others: as no less than Brahman. And not just a part of Brahman, as it has no parts — but all of it. Spirituality, therefore, is not a turning away from the world but a change of mind about the world.

"Dwelling on externals increases the fruit of superfluous evil desires for all sorts of things, so wisely recognizing this fact, one should abandon externals and cultivate attention to one's true nature within."

~ Vivekacūḍāmaṇi (Verse 334)

Related to this, Śrī Sarada Devi, the wife of the Indian Saint Śri Ramakrishna advised:

"Do not find fault with others. Rather see your own faults. Learn to make the world your own. No one is a stranger, my child. The whole world is your own."

In Part 2, you will observe that knowing everything is Brahman forms the foundation of the yamas (ethical observances) – the first limb of Yoga. It is with this understanding that we are to interact with the world, in our jobs and with our families, etc.

For Self-Realization, however, it is necessary to turn one's attention away from objects, both external and internal (thoughts, desires, emotions), and rest or abide in the Self. This is why the higher limbs of yoga are necessary, such as: withdrawal of the senses (Pratyāhāra); concentration (Dhāraṇā); and meditation (Dhyāna).

When Śrī Ramana Maharshi was asked*: *"How is God to be seen?"* he replied: *"Within. If the mind is turned inwards, God manifests as the inner consciousness."*

To which the questioner asked: *"But isn't God in all the objects we see around us?"*

Śrī Ramana Maharshi gave the following reply: *"God is in everything and in the seer. Where can God be seen? He cannot be found outside. He should be felt within. To see the objects, mind is necessary, and to conceive God in them is only a mental operation. But that is not real. The consciousness within, purged of the mind, is felt as God."*

*Conversation recorded in the book *Conscious Immortality* by Paul Brunton.

As you are nearing the end of Part 1….

Dear reader, you have come a long way in your journey of Self-enquiry!

At the end of the introduction, I claimed that it is only by knowing (directly intuiting) the Self that the Self can eventually be permanently realised. I hope that you are beginning to become established in this knowledge.

There are just a few more chapters in Part 1 to go. You may wish to revisit some of these sections later — perhaps after going through Part 2. You will find that it is the practice of yoga (the eight limbs) itself that will put the theory in context, making it clear and relevant.

CHAPTER 10

Who Am I?

*"Talking of the 'witness' should not lead to the idea that
there is a witness and something else apart from him that he
is witnessing. The 'witness' really means the light that illumines
the seer, the seen and the process of seeing. Before, during and
after the triads of seer, seen and seeing, the illumination exists.
It alone exists always."* ~ Śri Ramana Maharshi [55]

WE USE the term Pure Awareness or Pure Consciousness (also sometimes referred to as Original Consciousness) for the Ātman because in non-dual Reality, there is nothing else to be aware or conscious of*. Swami Sivananda describes the need for the term cidābhāsa (reflected consciousness) in the following quote:

> *"Take no notice of the ego and its activities, but see only the light behind. The ego is the I-thought. The true 'I' is the Self."*
>
> ~ Śri Ramana Maharshi
> (Talks, 146)

> *"In reality, the intellect by itself, is devoid of consciousness
> and the Self is devoid of action; the word 'Knows' cannot
> be predicated of either of them on any reasonable ground
> whatsoever."* [56]

*Here I am referring specifically to Para or Nirguṇa Brahman (the sole Reality/Pāramārthika standpoint) which is non-dual and therefore devoid of all action such as knowing, witnessing, discrimination, etc.

The first part of the word cidābhāsa is derived from Cit which means Pure Consciousness (Ātman or Brahman). The second part (ābhāsa) means that which appears, looks like, reflects, or yields any unreal appearance. Cidābhāsa, therefore, means a reflection or appearance of Pure Consciousness. The reflected consciousness is always aware of itself plus other things.

Nirguṇa Brahman (Pure/Original Consciousness) is all-pervading because, in the non-dual Absolute Reality, it is all there is. But in the same way that the Vedāntic rope* can never be found in the non-existent snake (all is rope!); Nirguṇa Brahman is not truly in the subtle or physical matter making up the perceivable universe (all is Brahman!). Thus, Brahman is said to transcend the physical universe.

*The physical universe is only an appearance in, or superimposition on Brahman — the underlying Pure Consciousness. The metaphor for this given previously is that of mistaking a rope for a snake in the semi-darkness.

At the Vyāvahārika standpoint (empirical universe of multiplicity):

Our mind is made up of sufficiently subtle matter to reflect Pure Consciousness. It is this reflection that we term cidābhāsa. Pure (Original) Consciousness is the substratum or underlying reality which the mind, through Māyā, is superimposed on.

The background of awareness* first introduced in Chapter 1, is reflected consciousness (Cidābhāsa). And yet, this reflection of consciousness is essentially non-different to Pure Consciousness as it has no independent reality apart from it. This may be compared to experiencing reflected light from the moon, knowing it originates from the sun (or original light in this analogy).

*That which is aware (the Witness) of all sense perceptions,

> *"Cause and effect are intrinsically non-different. The exercise of the effort towards experiencing the Real, becomes itself the experience of the Real. Without knowing the Real we cannot move towards the Real, and knowing it is being it."*
>
> ~ Swami Krishnananda

thoughts, desires, memories, emotions, and the thought 'I'; and is also equally aware of the absence of sense perceptions, thoughts, desires, memories, emotions, and the thought 'I'.

As discussed in the preceding chapters, it is thoughts that constitute the mind. All thought is subtle matter and therefore inert. The mechanism by which the inert or insentient mind and body appear to be a conscious individual entity is through the 'contact' or association of the reflected consciousness (cidābhāsa) with the ego or I-thought. Swami Chinmayananda* described this association as 'unholy wedlock.'

Dṛg-Dṛśya-Viveka provides us with the analogy of a fire and heated iron ball. The iron ball takes on the property of heat because it is close to the hot fire. Similarly, the inert ego (I-thought) appears to be a conscious entity only because of its contact with reflected consciousness.

> *"In the opinion of the wise, the identity of the reflection (of consciousness) and of the ego is like the identity of the fire and the (heated) iron ball. The body having been identified with the ego (which has already identified itself with the reflection of Consciousness) passes for a conscious entity."* ~ Dṛg-Dṛśya-Viveka (Verse 7)

*Swami Chinmayananda (1916-1993) inspired the formation of the Chinmaya Mission which was formed to disseminate the teachings of Advaita Vedānta. He was initiated into sannyāsa (Hindu vow of renunciation) by Swami Sivananda. With Swami Sivananda's blessing, he undertook rigorous scriptural study with the great Vedāntic master, Tapovan Maharaj of Uttarkashi.

As long as we have a mind, Pure Consciousness will be reflected in it. Without reflected consciousness we would not feel sentient, aware or able to perceive things. Swami Nikhilananda explains in his commentary on Dṛg-Dṛśya-Viveka:

> *"They (ego and reflection of Consciousness) never separate themselves from each other so long as they are taken to be real. It is like the reflection of the sun in the water in a pot. The reflection can never separate itself from water. The reflection disappears only when the water pot ceases to be."* [57]

In the above metaphor, when the water pot ceases to be, what remains is pure sunlight. Similarly, when the mind is transcended at the point of Self-realization, Pure Consciousness (Nirguṇa Brahman) alone remains.

To help us understand this more deeply, Śri Ramakrishna further elaborates:

> *"There are ten pots filled with water, and the sun is reflected in them. How many suns are there? Ten reflected suns and one real sun. Now break nine pots. How many suns are there? One reflected sun and one real sun. Break the last pot and how many suns are there? Is it only the real sun? Actually what remains cannot be described. What Is, remains. How do you know that the sun you are looking at is the real sun unless there is a reflected sun?"*

Sāṁkhya's 'many Puruṣas' — a matter of perspective

In the metaphor described above, each pot plus water symbolizes a separate physical body and mind respectively. The sun represents Original Consciousness (Nirguṇa Brahman) and the sun's reflection in the water contained in the various pots represents reflected consciousness (cidābhāsa).

Sāṁkhya's doctrine of there being 'many Puruṣas' may be

understood from the perspective of the individual (or vyā-vahārika standpoint). From this perspective, Puruṣa is reflected consciousness: the background of awareness (I AM) — the witness of all experience.

In the metaphor described above, there are many reflections (as there are number of pots). Similarly, the one Pure Consciousness is reflected in the subtle body (mind) of all sentient beings. The quality of each reflection, however, differs as it is dependent on the nature or quality of the mind it is reflected in.

From the perspective of Absolute Reality, there is only One Pure (Original) Consciousness. The **one Self** that illumines the minds of all beings — the Supreme Puruṣa*.

*In his commentary to yoga sūtra 3.34, Śri Vyāsa clearly equates Puruṣa with Brahman.

Relevance of Cidābhāsa to Spiritual Practice

The purpose of yoga sād-hanā (the eight limbs of yoga described in Part 2) is to purify the mind of rajas and tamas*. As it does so, the mind becomes increasingly pure or sattvic, with very little rajas and tamas remaining. A more sattvic mind is a quiet and peaceful mind that easily tunes into one's inner Presence no longer continuously drowned out by the ego's shrieks or demands (the thought agitations and negative emotions caused by rajas and tamas).

> *"I pray: O adorable Lord! Make my mind pure. Free me from all impure thoughts. Make my mind as transparent as a crystal, pure as the Himalayan snow, brilliant as the shining mirror."*
>
> ~ Swami Sivananda

*Rajas and tamas cannot be completely destroyed as all three guṇas are inherently present in prakṛti, although they are in constant flux. For example, without tamas there would be no sleep, etc; and without rajas, there would be no blood circulation, etc.

As the 'dirt' of rajas and tamas in the mind is removed through the various practices of yoga, the mind can be likened to a polished mirror or transparent crystal. The result is that the reflected consciousness becomes almost identical to the Original Consciousness (Nirguṇa Brahman or 'I-I').

This is the subject of the following quote by Ādi Śaṅkarācārya:

"The Self shines by the light of its own consciousness. When the intellect becomes extremely pure and transparent, its nature is similar to the nature of the Self. This is similar to how a crystal reflects the light of the sun". [58]

At this level of purity, one's mind may be compared to a thin layer of transparent glass or crystal that stands in the way of Reality (Pure Consciousness). There now arises a higher level of discrimination as the yogi intuits that one's real nature is the Original Consciousness that is utterly independent of the mind, but that by which the mind is revealed. The term Patañjali gives for this level of discrimination is viveka-khyāti.

In his commentary on the yoga sūtras, Śri Vyāsa emphasizes that viveka-khyāti is not to be taken as the goal of yoga. Even this knowledge (the discrimination of the difference between the intellect and Puruṣa) is a cognitive act and must be finally renounced for kaivalya (final liberation).

Rather, Patañjali (in yoga sūtra 2.26) specifies viveka-khyāti to be the means to liberation. And in yoga sūtra 2.28, Patañjali tells us that viveka-khyāti is obtained by putting into practice the eight limbs of yoga. It is the latter which destroys rajas and tamas in the inner instrument (mind and intellect) resulting in the viveka-khyāti that ultimately destroys ignorance. At which point, the now purified mind permanently dissolves into its Source, the Pure Consciousness.

In yoga sūtra 3.55, it is said:

"When the purity of the intellect is equal to that of Puruṣa [Pure Consciousness], kaivalya ensues." [59]

Who Am I?

Self-enquiry is fundamentally an investigation into 'Who Am I?' It is the process by which we uncover our true identity. We have thus far identified three I's*, only one of which is our real permanent identity: Nirguṇa Brahman or 'I-I'.

> *"To become free, your attention must be drawn to the 'I am,' the witness."*
>
> ~ Śri Nisargadatta Maharaj[60]

*In this discussion these are referred to as: 'I-I'; I AM; and I-thought.

The false 'I' is the ego or imposter self (I-thought) – that which identifies with the body and mind and says, 'I am hungry', 'I am a doctor', etc. This is referred to as 'the transient I' in the following quote:

"That which rises and falls is the transient 'I'. That which has neither origin nor end is the permanent I-I consciousness."
~ Śri Ramana Maharshi [61]

The awareness (reflected consciousness) which stands as the unchanging witness of the body and mind, is the 'I AM'

In order to realize the 'I-I', you must turn your attention to the 'I AM'.

Imagine finding yourself in a large, darkened room with only one small window covered by a thick drape or curtain, through which a faint ray of light enters. Nothing else is visible; it is so dark that not even the walls or door to the room can be seen. To reach direct sunlight on the other side of the drape, your only choice is to turn towards the faint ray of light, knowing it to have **no independent reality** from its source of direct sunlight.

The method for turning one's attention to the I AM is described in Chapter 5. You will find out experientially that the more Self-attentive you become, the brighter the 'light' of the Self becomes.

Keeping the Mind Sattvic

Patañjali provides us with a wonderful method for keeping the mind sattvic whilst engaging with others in the world. In yoga sūtra 1.33, he classifies all individuals into four categories, those who are: happy; sorrowful; virtuous; and wicked. He then advocates how one should endeavour to behave towards each type of person.

"Through cultivation of friendliness, compassion, joy and indifference to pleasure and pain, virtue and vice respectively, the consciousness becomes favourably disposed, serene and benevolent." [62]

In his commentary on this sūtra, B.K.S Iyengar remarks:

"Patañjali here lays the groundwork for our journey towards Self-Realization."

CHAPTER 11

Īśvara — God in the Dream of Separation

"You must worship the Self in Krishna,
not Krishna as Krishna." ~ Swami Vivekananda

"Christ has no body now, but yours.
No hands, no feet on Earth, but yours.
Yours are the eyes through which Christ
looks compassion into the world.
Yours are the feet with which Christ
walks to do good. Yours are the hands with
which Christ blesses the world."
~ Saint Teresa of Avila

ĪŚVARA (GOD), defined in Advaita Vedānta as Brahman plus Māyā, is equivalent to the God of religion, the Supreme Lord.

> *"In the secondless principle, Brahman, the whole universe, in the form of Īśvara and Jiva and all animate and inanimate objects, appears like a dream."*
>
> ~ Pañcadaśī (Verse VI.211)

For spiritual seekers, Īśvara has a crucial role to play. This is to help us wake up from the dream of separation to the Reality that, in truth, we never left.

In his commentary to The Moksha Gita by Swami Sivananda, Swami Krishnananda explains:

"He (Īśvara) is in a sense, the mediator between Jiva and Brahman. Here is the necessity of the Jivas for developing devotion to God, for a sudden jump into the infinite Brahman

is hard for the ignorant Jivas, without the help of the Universal Controller, Īśvara."

As Reality (Nirguṇa Brahman) is Pure Undifferentiated Consciousness, it is only from the Vyāvahārika standpoint (empirical or perceived universe) where discussion related to the triad of individual (jiva), world (jagat), and God (Īśvara) is relevant and required in order to make sense of our experience of separation. Śri Ramana Maharshi expressed this as follows:

"What exists in truth is the Self alone. The world, the individual soul, and God are appearances in it like silver in mother-of-pearl. These three appear at the same time, and disappear at the same time. The Self is that where there is absolutely no "I" thought. That is called 'Silence'."* [63]

*In this quote, the appearance of the world, individual soul and God are said to appear (and disappear) at the same time. Everything occurred (and still does within the dream of separation) simultaneously in a non-linear fashion. This cannot be understood by our linear programmed brain, hence why a staged model of creation is typically given.

In Chapter 8 I described how the impossible seemed to happen — an idea of separation or wish to create appeared to enter into Brahman. This thought instantaneously 'gave birth' to Prakṛti — the disturbance in which Pure Consciousness gets reflected.

The Vedāntic definition of Prakṛti is given in the following quote from Pañcadaśī:

> *"One alone exists.*
> *It appears as nature*
> *[Seen] and Soul [Seer]."*
>
> ~ Swami Vivekananda

*"Prakṛti (i.e. primordial substance) is that in which there is the reflection of Brahman, that is pure consciousness and bliss and is composed of sattva, rajas and tamas (in a state of homogeneity). **It is of two kinds.**"* ~ Verse I.15

The two kinds of Prakṛti are: (i) Sattva sullied with Rajas and Tamas; and (ii) pure Sattva.

Accordingly, Īśvara (Saguṇa Brahman) is both: (i) the material cause of the world; and (ii) the Cosmic Seer. In his commentary on The Bhagavad Gītā, Swami Sivananda explains:

> *"Just as the mind is the material cause and also the seer (Draṣṭā) for the objects seen in a dream, so also Īśvara is the material cause for this world (Upādāna-Kāraṇa) and also the Seer (Draṣṭā). He is also the efficient or the instrumental cause (Nimitta-Kāraṇa)."* [64]

Īśvara, the material cause of the world has already been described in Chapter 8: the cosmic causal body that transforms itself into the entire physical universe constituted of inert matter/energy ('nature' or the 'Seen'). We observed how there are an infinite variety of causal bodies due to the infinite combinations of sattva, rajas and tamas thus giving rise to the world of multiplicity.

The Pure Consciousness that gets reflected in the second type of Prakṛti (pure Sattva) is the consciousness/awareness principle ('Seer').

Absolute Reality or Nirguṇa Brahman (Pure Consciousness) is without attributes. Yet associated, as it were, with Māyā, it manifests as Seer and Seen.

In chapter 7 of the Bhagavad Gītā, Lord Krishna refers to these two aspects (Consciousness principle and material principle) as his higher (parā) and lower (aparā) natures respectively, and said of them:

> *"Know that these two (Natures) are the womb of all beings.*
> *As I am the source and dissolution of the whole universe."*
> ~ Verse 7.6

Yet, we also know experientially that everything 'seen' is ephemeral — an appearance only, and therefore ultimately unreal

(Mithyā). Lord Krishna, therefore, tells us to identify with His higher (parā) nature:

"the very life-element, by which this world is upheld."

~ Verse 7.5

At the level of the individual or jiva, this 'life-element' is our consciousness or awareness (Puruṣa).

At the cosmic level, Īśvara is the Cosmic Seer: consciousness or awareness associated with all beings.

When Arjuna asked Lord Krishna to grant him vision of his Cosmic form (Virāt), he was shown the entire physical manifestation of the universe

> *"Before the projection of the world the Supreme Self, the secondless, all-bliss and ever complete, alone existed. Through His Māyā He became the world and entered into it as the Jiva, the individual Self.*
>
> *Entering the superior bodies like that of Vishnu, He became the deities; and remaining in the inferior bodies like that of men He worships the deities."*
>
> ~ Pañcadaśī (Verses X.1 & X.2)

as one gigantic body of the Lord. This induced in him both wonder and terror. Quoting from the Bhagavad Gītā:

"I see Thee of boundless form on every side with many arms, stomachs, mouths and eyes: neither the end nor the middle nor also the beginning do I see, O Lord of the universe, O Cosmic Form." ~ Verse 11.16

Īśvara, the All-Knowing Cosmic Seer, is the Īśvara as defined by Patañjali. Patañjali describes Īśvara as a 'special Puruṣa', thus referring to the consciousness principle (Lord Krishna's higher nature)*. This definition** is arguably the most relevant one to our daily spiritual practice of meditation, etc.

*The yoga doctrine is that Īśvara is a particular Puruṣa, separate to the other (many) Puruṣas. That there are many Puruṣas is refuted by Ādi Śaṅkarācārya in his commentary on the yoga sūtras. For example: *"But Puruṣas being attributeless* *cannot conceivably be different in their own nature."*

**In Vedānta, Saguṇa Brahman (Īśvara) is also the efficient (intelligent) and material cause of the universe. According to Sāṁkhya, creation is solely the work of Prakṛti. This position (of Sāṁkhya) is refuted through logic in The Brahma Sūtras.

> **"As a person with a special nature, Īśvara rules the universe. Without His rulership there would be no one to regulate bondage and release."**
>
> ~ Pañcadaśī (Verse VI.106)

Through deep reflection, we begin to intuit our oneness with God. The substratum of reality, of both Īśvara (the Cosmic Seer) and the Jiva (individual), is the same one Pure or Original Consciousness (Nirguṇa Brahman). This is expressed by Swami Sivananda in the following quote:

"The one Cit (pure Consciousness) alone, reflected in a two-fold way, goes under the names of Īśvara and Jiva."* [65]

*Pure Consciousness reflected in pure sattva; and sattva sullied with rajas and tamas.

To join with God (Īśvara) is to abide in the Self in the understanding that we share the same ground of reality, which is Pure Consciousness.

The Christian mystic Meister Eckhart said:

"The eye through which I see God is the same eye through which God sees me; my eye and God's eye are one eye, one seeing, one knowing, one love."

The oneness of the Self with God is also the subject of the following quotes from various wisdom traditions:

"Whosoever knows his Self knows his Lord."

~ Prophet Muhammad

"Dwell in peace in the home of your own being, and the Messenger of Death will not be able to touch you."

~ Guru Nanak, founder of Sikhism

"Be still and know I AM God!" ~ Psalm 46:10

"Jesus said, The kingdom of God is within you." ~ Luke 17:21

"And God said to Moses, I AM THAT I AM. And He said Thus you shall say to the children of Israel, I AM has sent me to you." ~ Exodus 3.14

Lastly, Īśvara is the efficient (intelligent) or instrumental cause (Nimitta-Kāraṇa) of the World — the all-knowing agent that wields Māyā (His/Her creative power or Śakti) to bring the universe into manifestation.

The great mystic Śri Ramakrishna described Māyā in terms of both its deluding power (Avidyā Māyā) and liberating power (Vidyā Māyā). Of Māyā he explained:

> *"The Vidyā Māyā takes man towards God, whereas the Avidyā Māyā leads him astray. Knowledge, devotion, dispassion, compassion – all these are expressions of Vidyā Māyā; only with their help can one reach God."*

> *"It is Māyā that reveals Brahman. Without Māyā, who could have known Brahman? Without knowing Śakti, the manifested power of God, there is no means of knowing Him."*

> *"It is only due to Māyā that the attainment of supreme knowledge and final beautitude becomes possible for us. Otherwise who could even dream of all this? From Māyā alone spring duality and relativity; beyond Māyā there is neither the enjoyer nor the object of enjoyment."*

On a practical note

Iśvara, the Cosmic Seer, is omniscient (all-knowing). As a result of Iśvara's purity (Pure Consciousness reflected in Sattva), He/She is One and of supreme intelligence. Īśvara is described in yoga sūtra 1.24 as free of conflicts, unaffected by actions, and untouched by the law of karma. He/She is also described as: all wise; the first, foremost and absolute guru; and beyond time and space (yoga sūtras 1.25 and 1.26).

Īśvara's infinite wisdom and omniscience is symbolized by the five faces of the Hindu deity, Lord Śiva, described in the following quote from the book, *Radha — Diary of a Woman's Search* by Swami Sivananda Radha, a direct disciple of Swami Sivananda.

> *"He (Lord Śiva) can see with four faces to all corners of the world, and with the fifth he can see below and above. The eye of righteousness does not miss anything. His ears can listen to the four corner of the world and he can hear the inner unspoken secrets. Nothing is lost to the law of karma, neither the good nor the bad."*

A key point to understand in our spiritual practice is that Īśvara is free from ignorance (avidyā). In addition to knowing everything in the illusory universe, Īśvara also knows what we are in truth — Nirguṇa Brahman. Īśvara is that infinite wisdom that knows our best path to awakening — the specific lessons and experiences required for Self-realization.

Īśvara is the Inner Controller guiding the activities of all beings from within – indeed the entire Cosmos itself. This is the subject of the following quotes:

> *"He is the Lord of all; he is the knower of all; He is the controller within."* ~ Māṇḍūkya Upaniṣad (Verse VI)

> *"Know, then, that Prakṛti is Māyā and that the Great God is the Lord of Māyā. The whole universe is filled with objects which are parts of His being."* ~ Śvetāśvatara Upaniṣad (Verse IV. 10)

> *"The non-dual and resplendent Lord is hidden in all beings. All-pervading, the inmost Self of all creatures, the impeller to actions, abiding in all things, He is the Witness, the Animator, and the Absolute, free from guṇas."* ~ Śvetāśvatara Upaniṣad (Verse I. 11)

"Under Me as supervisor, Nature produces the moving and the unmoving; because of this, O Arjuna, the world revolves."
~ Bhagavad Gītā (Verse 9.10)

In order to help us wake up from the dream of separation, Īśvara may choose to extend love or truth into the illusory world. This may be through inspired thought and possibly visions of divine forms, but this always depends on the needs of the individual.

As described in Chapter 8, the physical world is a projection of the cosmic mind through the power of Māyā. It is the stream of thoughts arising from ignorance (avidyā), that turns the wheel of karma. Such thoughts are based on one's

> *"From the determination of Īśvara to create, down to His entrance into the created objects, is the creation of Īśvara. From the waking state to ultimate release, the cause of all pleasures and pains, is the creation of Jiva."*
>
> ~ Pañcadaśī (Verse VI.213)

likes, dislikes, attachments and fears, all of which arise from the mistaken belief that the body and world are real.

On the subject of karma, Śri Sarada Devi said*:

"No Doubt, God alone has become all these objects, animate and inanimate, but in the relative world all beings act and suffer according to their past karma and innate tendencies."

*Recorded in *Śri Sarada Devi, the Holy Mother, Her Teachings and Conversations*; translated by Swami Nikhilananda.

Ignorance (avidyā), and thus karma (the law of cause and effect), is beginningless. Yet, for all jivas (individuals), ignorance must come to an end, as it is Īśvara's supreme will that we realize the Self.

Yoga sūtra 2.22 tells us:

"The relationship with nature ceases for emancipated beings, its purpose having been fulfilled, but its processes continue to affect others."* [66]

*This yoga sūtra is from the perspective of the jiva (unenlightened person).

Thus, when we surrender to God (Īśvara), by His/Her grace, the entire universe will conspire to help us quicken our journey home. The sole purpose of the Seen (nature or prakṛti) is to provide the necessary experiences for that purpose. This is the subject of yoga sūtra 2.21:

"Nature and intelligence exist solely to serve the seer's true purpose, emancipation." [67]

We must remember that God's Grace comes only to those that invite it. **This is the practical aspect.** We must be proactive. By identifying with the Self within we are making the choice of Perfect Oneness (Reality) over the dream of separation.

Alternatively, if we continue to turn our back on the Absolute and make the dream of separation real, the endless cycle of birth and death, with all its pleasures and pains, will continue. Yoga sūtra 2.18 makes it clear that the choice is ours:

"Nature, its three qualities, sattva, rajas and tamas, and its evolutes, the elements, mind, senses of perception and organs of action, exist externally to serve the seer, for enjoyment or emancipation".* [68]

*Bhoga here is translated as enjoyment. In other translations of the yoga sutras, bhoga is translated as 'experience'.

> *"The Vedānta is the most satisfactory system of philosophy. It has been evolved out of the Upaniṣads. It has superseded all other schools."*
>
> ~ Swami Sivananda[69]

Sāṁkhya Superseded by Vedānta?

Sāṁkhya and Yoga are two of the six schools of Hindu philosophy (darśanas) and are traditionally linked together.

Sāṁkhya (and Yoga by association), is a dualistic philosophy. In Sāṃkhya cosmology, Puruṣa and Prakṛti are two independent and parallel realities. In contrast, Prakṛti as defined by Vedānta does not have any independent existence apart from Brahman (see Chapter 8).

When we begin to examine Sāṃkhya's dualistic notion that Puruṣa and Prakṛti are two independent and parallel realities; we can first observe that this philosophical system did not benefit from the Vedāntic doctrine of the different tiers of 'truth'. It is more reasonable, therefore, to consider Sāṃkhya's teachings at the vyāvahārika standpoint (perceived or empirical reality). From this standpoint, dualistic language is necessary to explain the jivas (our) dualistic experience, that of the Seer (consciousness principle or Puruṣa) and the Seen (Prakṛti).

Ultimately, Sāṃkhya and Vedānta have the very same goal, even though different words are used to describe it. Just as Vedānta aims at destroying ignorance, the aim of Sāṃkhya is to remove Aviveka, non-discrimination between the Seer and the Seen. The result of both is direct knowledge of the Absolute. Sāṃkhya's transcendental aloneness (Kaivalya) – in which there remains only Puruṣa – is no different to the Advaitic Realization of Para Brahman. They are referring to the same Pure Undifferentiated Consciousness.

Raja Yoga (Patañjali's yoga sūtras), provides us with the theoretical basis for meditation. The sole aim of the eight limbs of yoga is to prepare the mind to be able to enter into asaṃprajñātā samādhi (known also as nirvikalpa samādhi), not as a temporary ecstatic state, but to attain final liberation (Kaivalya).

Therefore, although its philosophical basis is dualistic, Raja Yoga helps us to wake-up to non-dual Reality. On this subject Swami Sivananda explained:

"Though Raja Yoga is a dualistic philosophy and treats of Prakṛti and Puruṣa, it helps the student in Advaitic Realization of oneness eventually. Though there is the mention of

*Puruṣa, ultimately the Puruṣa becomes identical with Highest
Self or Puruṣa, or Brahman of Upaniṣads. Raja Yoga pushes
the student to the highest rung of the spiritual ladder of
Advaitic realization of Brahman."* [70]

And yet, Sāṁkhya philosophy has been greatly superseded
by the much more satisfactory system of Advaita Vedānta.

In a talk on 'The absolute and manifestation' given in London
in 1896, Swami Vivekananda claimed that of all the systems, Advaita Vedānta has the greatest appeal in the modern age:

*"I may make bold to say that the only religion which agrees
with, and even goes a little further than modern researchers,
both on physical and moral lines is the Advaita, and that is
why it appeals to modern scientists so much. They find that
the old dualistic theories are not enough for them, do not
satisfy their necessities. A man must have not only faith,
but intellectual faith too".*

Similarly, Swami Sivananda advised:

*"During the time of Śaṅkaracharya, all six schools of philoso-
phy flourished, Therefore, he had to refute the other systems
in order to establish his absolute monism (kevala Advaita).
But, nowadays, Sāṁkhya, Vaiśeṣika, etc., are in name only.
Even now, some Hindu preachers, Sannyasins and Manda-
lesvars try to establish Advaita Vedānta by refuting these
old systems. This is a mistake. They will have to refute at
the present moment: materialism, agnosticism, atheism
and science, and then establish Advaita Vedānta."* [71]

The greater appeal of Advaita Vedānta lies in how this
school of thought developed particularly during the lifetime of
Ādi Śaṅkarācārya.

One of the main areas of development in Vedānta around
the time of Ādi Śaṅkarācārya was the doctrine of Māyā and superimposition. In his introduction to The Upaniṣads Volume I,

Swami Nikhilandanda comments that although the doctrine of Māyā can be traced to the Ṛgveda, it was later developed by Vedāntists including Śrī Vyāsa, Śrī Gaudapāda and Ādi Śankarācārya. In addition, these teachings emphasized the two tiers of reality or truth (vyāvahārika and pāramārthika).

Of Ādi Śankarācārya, Swami Sivananda explained:

"Śankara was the exponent of the Kevala Advaita philosophy [unqualified non-dualism]. His teachings can be summed up in the following words:

Brahman alone is real, this world is unreal; the Jiva is identical with Brahman.

Śankara preached Vivarta Vāda [apparent transformation]. Just as the snake is superimposed on the rope, this world and this body are superimposed on Brahman or the Supreme Self. If you get a knowledge of the rope, the illusion of the snake will vanish. Even so, if you get a knowledge of Brahman, the illusion of the body and the world will vanish."[72]

Pause for Reflection

Before we proceed to the next chapter, let us reflect for a moment on the fact that nothing can actually be destroyed by Self-enquiry/Self-knowledge except ignorance. Whenever I use the terms 'destroy' or 'annihilate', the meaning should always be taken to be figurative. We have already seen that the world(s) of names and forms (including the body and mind) is nothing apart from You, the Pure Awareness.

When we first begin Self-enquiry, it is not uncommon for us to feel a sense of unease or even fear. If you do, my advice is that you connect with the core of your being and from this safe and quiet centre observe any emotions that come up. Although you should not deny them, please remember that these emotions and feelings are all objects of your awareness. They are not your real, permanent nature.

Certainly, courage is a needed on the spiritual path! Especially as we begin to come to terms with the loss of individuality associated with Self-realization, the subject of the next chapter.

Śri Ramana Maharshi, in the following quote, uses a beautiful analogy of letting go or losing hold of a branch of a tree: one gains nothing by holding precariously onto the branch yet gains the ALL by courageously being able to let go.

"Do not doubt, with fear, what will happen when you completely lose your individuality. The true State of Self will then Itself be yours, just as one will permanently remain firm on the ground when one loses one's hold on the branch of a tree."
~ Guru Vachaka Kovai (Verse 354)

CHAPTER 12

The Uncomfortable Truth

"He longs to be free....
He has no care for this world
Or the next,
And he knows what is passing
Or forever.
And yet how strange!
He is still afraid of freedom."
~ Aṣṭāvakra Gītā [73]

"Then Jesus said to his disciples, 'Whoever wants to be
my disciple must deny themselves and take up their cross and
follow me. For whoever wants to save their life will lose it,
but whoever loses their life for me will find it.'"
~ Matthew 16:24–25

IN THE classic Vedāntic metaphor of the snake and the rope (introduced in Chapter 8), it is clear that the appearance of the snake is dependent on the rope; unless a rope exists, the illusory sighting of a snake cannot occur. The rope, however, is in no way dependent on the non-existent snake.

Similarly, the appearance of the physical world depends on Para Brahman, the underlying reality. Yet Brahman itself remains unaffected by the appearance, in the same way that sand in the dessert remains unaffected by the water seen in a mirage.

Lord Krishna tells us:

"Whatever beings (and objects) that are pure, active and
inert, know that they proceed from Me. They are in Me,*

yet I am not in them." ~ Bhagavad Gītā (Verse 7.12)

*Here, Lord Krishna is referring to matter consisting of the three Guṇas (sattva, rajas and tamas).

At first glance the above verse appears to contradict Lord Krishna's earlier teachings that he is the Self in all beings. In his commentary on the Bhagavad Gītā, Swami Sivananda adds the following explanation to this verse:

"Though these beings and objects proceed from Me, I am not in them; they are in me. I am independent. I am the support for them; they depend on Me just as the superimposed snake depends on the rope. The snake is in the rope, but the rope is never in the snake."

Similarly, Brahman can never be in the world, or even be remotely aware of it, because from the standpoint of Nirguṇa Brahman, there is no world.

From this standpoint, not only does the world not exist, the ultimate truth is that you and I do not exist at any other level except as Pure Undifferentiated Consciousness.

In Chapter 10 I explained that up to the point of Self-realization, Brahman can only be experienced indirectly as reflected consciousness.

I also described how, through the practice of yoga, the mind becomes increasingly pure or sattvic. As a result, the reflected consciousness becomes increasingly identical to the Original Consciousness. But even this is not Self-realization.

The daunting fact is that your experience as an individual (plus the world) and Nirguṇa Brahman (Absolute Reality) are mutually exclusive — you cannot have both. At some point, you must choose. To realize Brahman, your individuality must be permanently relinquished.

However, Self-realization does not mean death of the physical body. Otherwise spiritual seekers throughout the ages would not have benefited from the teachings of Saints and Self-realized masters. This apparent paradox is discussed in the next chapter.

To give some reassurance:

Self-realization is not about giving anything up. It is about being given everything — all of Reality, an infinite ocean of Bliss. The real you, and the real essence of all your loved ones, is forever in existence, only as Perfect Oneness.

> *"Keep on remembering 'I am neither the mind nor its ideas.' Do it patiently and with conviction and you will surely come to the direct vision of yourself as the source of being – knowing — loving, eternal, all-embracing, all-pervading. You are the infinite focused in a body. Now you see the body only. Try earnestly and you will come to see the infinite only."*
>
> ~ Śri Nisargadatta Maharaj[74]

Ādi Śaṅkarācārya in his commentary on the Kaṭha Upaniṣad (Verse II.ii.14.) refers to the bliss of Self-realization and how it is worth striving for:

> *"The bliss that arises from the realization of the Self is no doubt beyond thought and speech, which belong to relative existence; but it is directly experienced by illumined souls. Therefore, one should not give up the efforts for Self-realization as impossible; one should rather strive with faith and reverence."*

I am bringing up "the uncomfortable truth" now, before we move on to Part 2, in recognition of the possibility of ego resistance or sabotage. Śri Nisargadatta Maharaj warns:

> *"It is the mind that tells you that the mind is there. Don't be deceived. All the endless arguments about the mind are produced by the mind itself, for its own protection, continuation and expansion. It is the blank refusal to consider the convolutions and convulsions of the mind that can take you beyond it."* [75]

The required loss of one's individuality for final liberation is the subject of verses 2 to 4 in Chapter VII of The Moksha Gita by Swami Sivananda. The following quote is Swami Krishnananda's (a direct disciple of Swami Sivananda) beautifully majestic commentary on these verses. Please take the time to read it, as some degree of reflection is required.

> *"In the light of the all-ness of Brahman the great denial of the world ensues. The mind in its static aspect is Brahman itself, but in its dynamic aspect appears as the world. The knowledge of this fact withdraws the faith in the external universe into the Bhuma*, where nothing else is. The citadel of individuality is broken by the invasion of the Absolute. The life of misery and risk in the world is stepped over only through the sacrifice of the separate self. One who gives away the all, gets the All. The charity of the self brings the fruit of Absoluteness and Immortality. The complete possession of everything that exists is possible only by effacing oneself completely. The person who ties his thoughts to that which is beyond the ego loses his ego. The self must be lost if the Self is to be gained. The removing of the veil is the removing of one's own personality, and the higher Truth is realized in proportion to the extent to which the lower individuality is suppressed. A veritable suicide of the ego is what is meant by the dissolution of personality in Eternity. It is like cutting the branch of a tree by sitting on that branch itself. The slow self-transcendence practiced through Yoga and Wisdom leads the aspirant to the Heart of Bliss where his thirst is quenched forever, and the hunger of ages appeased!"*

*Bhuma is a term referring to Brahman — where nothing else is seen or heard.

Self-realization may thus seem like an impending death, a loss of all that we know and hold dear. At some point in our spiritual practice, for example during a deep meditation, there may be a sense that we are approaching a threshold or door to what seems like oblivion. This is articulated below in a quote by Jan Frazier:

> *"Many spiritual seekers who say their wish is to awaken don't actually want what they believe they do. This becomes clear sometimes at the approach to the brink of what feels like a void, where the obliteration of the egoic self seems imminent. With a shocked recognition of what is being asked, the person will recoil. The scale of the loss — the dissolution of the familiar self — is beyond what was bargained for."* [76]

Further clarification is also given in this quote by Dr David Hawkins, from his book *Reality and Subjectivity*:

> *"The underpinnings of the ego are its illusion that it is a separate self and that the perceptions which its positionality produces are real. When these structures are transcended, the ego brings up its last reserves. These consist of the threat of death or the threat of facing the total void of nothingness or nonexistence. When this arises, it becomes rapidly clear that one is now forced to make a decision and choose.*
>
> *Into this gap in the flow of consciousness there will arrive, beyond conscious recall, the knowingness of the Sage, the Bodhisattva, the Teacher, the Avatar, the knowing-ness of the Enlightened beings of all times. Instructions will be known:*
>
> *'Hold back nothing; completely surrender life itself to God. Be willing to experience death. Refuse the void, for it is merely another illusion of the ego and has no reality. Truth has no opposite.'*
>
> *Faith in teachings of those who have realized the Truth is crucial. They spring forth into awareness and strengthen the willingness to surrender and to experience the death that is*

*simultaneously the birth of the Self. By invitation and
surrender, death becomes an experiential reality. It can
be fearful and intimidating for a brief moment. It is not
like the physical deaths that occurred in previous incar-
nations when one left the body with great relief. This is
actually the first and also the last time that real death
can be experienced. Therefore, it need be gone though
only one time ever.*

*With the courage of conviction and the inspiration of
the Self and its teachers, one surrenders to the plunge. For
a few moments, the last great fear erupts, and one experiences what it really means to die completely as the great
door swings open to the Splendor, beyond all comprehension.*

*The Presence reveals that the Infinite Splendor is actually
one's own Self."*

Although I have referred to the subject of this chapter as 'the
uncomfortable truth', it is only uncomfortable in proportion to
how much we identify with the body and mind/intellect and
view the world of external objects as real.

The more you turn your attention toward the Self, and
thereby lessen your identification with your false identity, the
greater will be your conviction that your real identity is forever
in existence and cannot be threatened in any way.

Awakening to Reality is meant to be a gentle, graceful process, and one that will only result in great joy and peace, even as
you continue to act normally in the world.

It is also reassuring to remember that it is only you yourself
who can make the decision to loosen and finally let go of your grip
on the branch of this tree of saṃsāra. As soon as you begin to loos-
en your grip, even a little, you will be helped by God's infinite grace.

In the next and final chapter of Part 1, we will further examine what it means to transcend the body and mind and permanently realize the Self.

CHAPTER 13

Manonāśa — When the Mind Becomes No-mind

"This world-illusion has arisen because of the movement of thought in the mind; when that ceases the illusion will cease too, and the mind becomes no-mind."
~ Yoga-Vāsiṣṭha

VĀSANĀS are our innate tendencies or inclinations that arise as a result of the five kleśas (afflictions). The afflictions are: avidyā (ignorance); asmitā (individuality/egoism); rāga (intense likes, attachments); dveṣa (dislikes, special hates); and abhiniveśa (clinging to life, fear of death).

> *"What is this world, after all? It is nothing but the materialization of the thought-forms of Hiraṇyagarbha (cosmic mind)."*
> ~ Swami Sivananda[77]

The mind and intellect (the fabric of our personality) are a gross manifestation of our vāsanās. When a vāsanā comes into fruition it migrates from the causal body (kāraṇa śarīra) to the subtle body (sūkṣma śarīra) and produces a desire, from which arises thought (vṛtti). After a thought has arisen it does not disappear but leaves an impression or imprint (saṁskāra) in the sub-conscious mind, giving birth to new vāsanās. Thoughts propel us into action, further strengthening the vāsanās.

Swami Sivananda describes this cyclical nature of mental conditioning in the following quote:

"Vāsanā (desire in subtle form) is a wave in the mind-lake. Its seat is the Kāraṇa Sarīra (causal body). It exists there in the form of a seed and manifests in the mind-lake. Just as flowers are latent in seeds, Vāsanās are latent in the Antaḥkaraṇa and the Kāraṇa Sarīra (seed-body). Daily new flowers blossom out. They fade out in a day or two. Similarly, vāsanās blossom out like flowers one by one, come out to the surface of the mind, generate Sankalpas** in the mind of Jivas and goad them to strive to possess and enjoy the particular objects of enjoyment. Vāsanās cause actions, and actions strengthen the Vāsanās. This is a Chakra, vicious circle. On the advent of knowledge of Brahman, all Vāsanās are fried out. The real enemies are the Vāsanās within. Annihilate them. Eradicate them. They are inveterate."* [78]

*'Inner instrument' — primarily the mind and intellect (see page 29)

**A sankalpa is the notion of joy in an external object. From this arises desire.

The kleśas, therefore, are at the root of all our actions, and ignorance (avidyā) is the root of the other kleśas. As long as the kleśas exist, we will continue to experience the effects of karma. This is the subject of yoga sūtra 2.13:

"As long as the root of all actions exists, it will give rise to class of birth, span of life and experiences." [79]

The entire storehouse of an individual's vāsanās are the sanchita vāsanās. Out of these, the vāsanās that exert pressure for fulfillment in this life are the prārabdha vāsanās. It is the prārabdha vāsanās that have determined our current body and external environment in order that these desires may be realized and the good or bad effects of previous actions (karma) may take effect.

Important note!

You are not a victim of your vāsanās!

Human beings, unlike animals, have a unique capacity to choose their actions, regardless of one's innate tendencies or vāsanās.

By your right choice and subsequent action (in thought, word, and deed) in every present moment, unhelpful vāsanās to the goal of yoga are gradually eradicated.

It is through this self-effort that you can change your future destiny (prārabdha).

But for Self-realization, vāsanās have to be extinguished entirely. This is emphasized in the following two quotes:

"Even after the Truth has been realized, there remains that strong, beginningless, obstinate impression that one is the agent and experiencer, which is the cause of one's transmigration (re-birth). It has to be carefully removed by living in a state of constant identification with the supreme Self. ***Sages call that Liberation which is the extinction of Vāsanās (impressions) here and now."***

~ Vivekacūḍāmaṇi (Verse 267)

"Mind is a bundle of Vāsanās (subtle desires). Through Vāsanās bondage is caused. Destruction of Vāsanās will bring freedom. The mind will attain quiescence like a ghee-less lamp if the Vāsanās are destroyed."

~ Swami Sivananda, The Moksha Gita (Verses VI 2,3)

"There is no Ignorance (Avidyā) outside the mind. The mind alone is Avidyā, the cause of the bondage of transmigration. When that is destroyed, all else is destroyed, and when it is manifested, everything else is manifested."

~ Vivekacūḍāmaṇi (Verse 169)

In his commentary on Swami Sivananda's The Moksha Gita (verses VI 2,3), Swami Krishnananda compares the mind to a piece of cloth which, while appearing whole, consists entirely of threads.

> *"Just as cloth is nothing but a bundle of threads, the mind is nothing but a cluster of vāsanās or past impressions and subtle desires that persistently lurk within the subconscious. When the threads are pulled out one by one, where is cloth at all?"*
>
> *"When the threads of vāsanās are destroyed the cloth of the mind also disappears from existence. The Ambrosia of Brahman is drunk deep. The soul is drowned in the ocean of joy."*

When all one's vāsanās are eradicated, the mind becomes no-mind. Swami Sivananda explains:

> *"When the mind does not function owing to the absence of Vāsanās (mental impressions and subtle desires), then arises the state of Manonāśa or annihilation of the mind."* [80]

With Manonāśa, one attains final liberation or kaivalya. This is described by Swami Sivananda using the analogy of fire and its fuel:

> *"Just as the fire is absorbed into its source when the fuel is burnt out, so also, the mind is absorbed into its source, the Ātman, when all Sankalpas or thoughts are annihilated. Then one attains Kaivalya, the experience of the Timeless Reality, the state of absolute independence."* [81]

Manonāśa, however, does not mean annihilation of the Self. In his book *Mind — Its Mysteries and Control*, Swami Sivananda defines the meaning of Manonāśa:

> *"Destruction of egoism, Rāga-Dveṣa (attraction and repulsion for objects) and all Vāsanās alone is Manonāśa. Manonāśa means the death of the present form of the mind (i.e., the instinctive mind of emotions and passions), the form*

which perceives differences where none exists, which identi-
fies the Self with the body. Its death really means its transfor-
mation into and, therefore, the birth of cosmic consciousness."

How Are Vāsanās Destroyed?

By focus on that which is free from vāsanās: the Self.

In his great classic Vivekacūḍāmaṇi (Crest Jewel of Discrimination), Ādi Śaṅkarācārya tells us that vāsanās get extinct to the
extent to which the mind is absorbed in the Self. For example:

"When the mass of desires for things other than oneself
obscuring the contrary desire for one's real self are elimin-
ated by constant self-remembrance, then it discloses itself
of its own accord." ~ Verse 275

"As the mind become more and more inward-turned, it
becomes gradually freed from external desires, and when
all such desires are fully eliminated Self-realization is com-
pletely freed from obstruction." ~ Verse 276

"When he is always poised in Self-awareness the yogi's think-
ing mind stops, and the cessation of desires takes place as a
result, so see to the removal of all ideas of additions to your
true Self." ~ Verse 277

The result of being continuously Self-attentive is that
vāsanās get destroyed and karma gradually undone. Instead of
having to come back in possibly one million dream bodies, perhaps we only need to come back five or ten times, or perhaps
not at all!

Yoga sūtra 2.16 tells us:

*"The pains which are yet to come **can be and are to be***
avoided." [82]

Therefore, all progress made in this life, no matter how small,
is not wasted.

Lord Krishna assures us:

"There [in the next birth] he comes in touch with the knowledge acquired in his former body and strives more than before for perfection, O Arjuna." ~ Bhagavad Gītā (Verse 6.43)

Swami Sivananda adds in his commentary to this verse:

"The saṁskāras of Yogic practices and meditation and the Yogic tendencies will compel the spiritual aspirant to strive with greater vigour than that with which he attempted in his former birth. He will endeavor more strenuously to get more spiritual experiences and to attain to higher planes of realization than those acquired in his previous birth."

Conclusion to Part 1

In Part 1 of this book, my aim has been to help you establish contact with your Self — and to understand Pure Awareness to be not only your true nature, but the only Reality. This Pure Awareness is not something that needs to be gained. You already are it! It is here — everywhere — all the time!

Quoting Thomas Byrom, from his introduction to the Aṣṭāvakra Gītā, this summary may be articulated as follows:

"We are all one Self. The Self is pure awareness. This Self, this flawless awareness is God. There is only God*.*

Everything else is an illusion: the little self, the world, the universe. All these things arise with the thought 'I,' that is, with the idea of separate entity. The little 'I' invents the material world, which in our ignorance we strive hard to sustain. Forgetting our original oneness, bound tightly in our imaginary separateness, we spend our lives mastered by a specious sense of purpose and value. Endlessly constrained by our habit of individuation, the creature of preference and desire, we continually set one thing against another, until the mischief and misery of choice consume us.

But our true nature is pure and choiceless awareness. We are already and always fulfilled. 'It is easy,' says Aṣṭāvakra. 'You are the clear space of awareness (Cidākāśa), pure and still, in whom there is no birth, no striving, no I.'"

*Here 'God' is referring to Para Brahman.

Although we already are Pure Awareness or Pure Consciousness, we somehow overlook it... until it is pointed out to us during the act of yoga called Svādhyāya!

In the following quote, Śri Nisargadatta Maharaj refers to the blessings or grace that begins to flow as result of becoming Self-aware.

"The awareness that you are will open your eyes to what you are. It is all very simple. First of all, establish a contact with your Self, be with yourself all the time. Into Self-awareness all blessings flow." [83]

What are these blessings?

When we stand firmly in the knowledge of advaita: that behind the ever-changing appearance of the world there is a changeless substratum — the all-pervading Reality, we no longer become swayed by the endless ups and downs of the transactional world. You will discover for yourself that this is the secret to long-lasting happiness.

Also, by training the mind to introspect or look within (the focus of Part 2), it becomes calmer, with fewer agitations. As a result, you will receive more inspired thought concerning your daily life (work and family, etc) and the practical decisions you need to make. This may bring considerable success in worldly endeavours, although things will not necessarily always work out how you imagined. Blessings also come in the form of life's 'pin-pricks' or challenges, just so we do not forget what life is really about!

Pause for Reflection: Liberated Sages — a paradox or not?

We've examined how kaivalya (final liberation) is associated with Manonāśa — annihilation of the egoic mind consisting of vāsanās (desires in subtle form) and past impressions (saṁskāras).

But what about the apparent paradox of Self-realized sages such as Śrī Ramana Maharshi engaging with the world?

Let us first consider the phenomenon of liberated sages from the perspective of each of the two mutually exclusive standpoints (Pāramārthika and Vyāvahārika) described earlier.

Pāramārthika (Nirguṇa Brahman — Highest Reality or Truth). From this standpoint, the highest truth, expressed by Śrī Gaudapāda, is: *"There is neither dissolution nor creation, none in bondage and none practicing disciplines. There is none seeking Liberation and **none liberated**. This is the absolute truth."*
~ Māṇḍūkya Kārikā (Verse II.32)

Vyāvahārika (Empirical World Standpoint). We perceive a liberated sage (a jīvan-mukta or jñānī), living out his or her remaining prārabdha karma.

The conclusion: When we (ajñānī) see the body of a liberated sage (jñānī) such as Śrī Ramana Maharshi, it is because we are still dreaming. The sage has no awareness of the body or the world. Self-realization (kaivalya) is the awakening to Reality (Nirguṇa Brahman); not becoming more awake in the dream of separation.

From our (vyāvahārika) standpoint, the sage is perhaps best seen as God (Īśvara) in human form (inhabiting a body). It is by Īśvara's grace, as a result of good actions in previous births, that we have the good fortune to be in the company of such a being.

When a visitor asked Śrī Ramana Maharshi*, *"If all that we see is mere illusion, and no more real than a dream, what about the form before us, on the couch talking to us about Truth and*

Reality?" Then the visitor recalled:

"He (Śri Ramana Maharshi) remained silent for a few seconds. I repeated the question. He called for a Tamil book 'Ozhuvil Odukkam' and read out and explained the second verse in it, which said that a Jñāni is, to his disciple in jāgrat (our state of wakefulness), like a lion in the dream of a mad elephant. The dream lion startles and wakes up the elephant – the lion, the dream and the elephant vanishes and what is, remains. Even so the enlightened Guru wakes up the adept disciple to absolute Reality in which there is neither Guru or siśhya (disciple)."

*Recorded in Mountain Path, 1968, Page 89; "Wake Us Up", by R. Narayana Iyer.

Similarly, Śri Nisargadatta Maharaj was asked similar questions. One of his replies was:

"What do you know of me, when even my talk with you is in your world only?"

Ultimately, however, we should not be overly concerned with what happens to the world appearance on Self-realization or Kaivalya. Our focus now is to abide or rest in the Self until that alone becomes the solid Reality. Śri Ramana Maharshi indicates this in the following answer recorded in Maharshi's Gospel:

"Why worry yourself about the world and what happens to it after Self-realization? First realise the Self. What does it matter if the world is perceived or not? Do you gain anything to help you in your quest by the non-perception of the world during sleep? Conversely, what would you lose now by the projection of the world? It is quite immaterial to the jñāni or ajñāni if he perceives the world or not."* [84]

*Once established in kaivalya – the timeless Reality.

Below are additional quotes from several Self-realized sages, all from the Pāramārthika standpoint (Nirguṇa Brahman, the highest and only Reality).

If there are two or three (or more) quotes that you are particularly drawn to, please use them for contemplation. These are all quotes that you can contemplate again and again.

When reading the quotes, it is important to bear in mind that use of phrases such as 'disappearance of the universe' (on final liberation) is figurative. From the Pāramārthika standpoint, as there is no world, neither can it actually disappear. Śrī Gaudapāda explains:

"If the phenomenal universe were real, then certainly it would disappear. The universe of duality [which is cognized] is mere illusion (māyā); Non-duality alone is the Supreme Reality."
~ Māṇḍūkya Kārikā (Verse I.17)

On this verse of Śrī Gaudapāda's, Ādi Śaṅkarācārya comments:

"There is no doubt that the phenomenal universe would disappear if it really existed. But the duality known as the universe is māyā. The only real substance is Non-duality, which may be likened to the rope..."*

"Hence it stands to reason that there is no such thing as the coming into existence of the manifold universe or its destruction." [85]

*In the snake and rope analogy

The quotes:

"Just as a man does not behold the object which he has seen in his dream when he is awake, so also the Jīvanmukta does not perceive the universe after he attains knowledge of Brahman." ~ Swami Sivananda [86]

"Just as the spider emits the thread (of the web) out of itself and again withdraws it into itself, likewise the mind projects the world out of itself and again resolves it into itself. When

the mind leaves the Self, the world appears, Therefore, when the world appears, the Self does not appear; and when the Self appears (shines) the world does not appear."
~ Śri Ramana Maharshi [87]

"Your real state is the Self, and in that Self there is no body and no mind." ~ Śri Annamalai Swami [88]

"When one is firmly established in Self-knowledge, which is infinite, unlimited and unconditioned, then the delusion or ignorance that gave rise to the world-appearance comes to an end." ~ Yoga-Vāsiṣṭha

"Where has the world gone? Who has removed it, or where has it disappeared to? I saw it only just now, and now it is not there." ~ Vivekacūḍāmaṇi (Verse 483)

"So long as even a dreamlike awareness of yourself as an individual in the world remains, as a wise person persistently see to the removal of all ideas of additions to your true Self."
~ Vivekacūḍāmaṇi (Verse 285)

"How can there be distinctions in a supreme reality which is by nature one? Who has noticed any distinctions in the pure joy of deep sleep?" ~ Vivekacūḍāmaṇi (Verse 403)

"After realisation of the supreme Truth, all this no longer exists in one's true nature of the imageless God. The snake is not to be found in time past, present or future, and not a drop of water is to be found in a mirage." ~ Vivekacūḍāmaṇi (Verse 404)

"The Self, revealed as our true nature within the heart through the power of Self enquiry, is none other than the peerless reality of the Supreme, which alone remains after this worldly illusion has faded into nothingness."
~ Śri Muruganar [89]

*"Where there is duality, as it were, there one sees the other —
but where everything is one's own Self, then, whom would one
see?"* ~ Bṛhadāraṇyaka Upaniṣad (Verse II.iv.14)

*"Where one sees nothing else, hears nothing else, understands
nothing else, that is the Infinite."* ~ Chāndogya Upaniṣad (Verse
VII.24.1)

PART 2

YOGA

To the noblest of sages Patañjali
Who gave us Yoga for serenity of mind
Grammar for purity of speech
And medicine for perfection of the body, I bow
I prostrate before Patañjali
Whose upper body has a human form
Whose arms hold a conch and a disc
Who is crowned by a thousand headed cobra
O incarnation of Ādiśeṣa,
My salutations to Thee

"To behold the one Self in all beings is jñāna, wisdom;
to love the Self is Bhakti, devotion; to serve the Self
is Karma, action. Yoga supplies the method by which
the Self can be seen, loved and served."
~ Yoga of Synthesis by Swami Sivananda

PART 2 is about our sādhanā, the practice of yogic discipline, or Patañjali's eight limbs of yoga.

The eight limbs of yoga are:

Yamas (moral restraints); Niyamas (inner observances); Āsanas (seat or posture); Prāṇāyāma (control of vital energy); Pratyāhāra (withdrawal of the senses); Dhāraṇā (concentration); Dhyāna (meditation); and Samādhi (absorption in Brahman).

The aim of this section is not to reinterpret or analyze any of the sutras related to your yoga practice, but to examine how you may actually put into practice the yamas and niyamas, in addition to the higher limbs of yoga, such that their ultimate goal may be realised.

In order to fully transcend the body and mind, spiritual practice is essential. We should not delude ourselves for a moment in thinking that because we are already Brahman we need do nothing.

Aṣṭāvakra warns us:

> *"One-pointedness means focusing the mind on God alone, freeing it from all attractions towards objects of this Māyā-Bazaar and making it go inward instead of outward. This is the secret, and Viveka (discrimation) and Vichāra (enquiry) are the prerequisites for attaining such Ekāgratā or one-pointedness. This must be practiced daily, constantly – it is called abhyāsa, it is called Yoga."*
>
> ~ Swami Chidananda

"The moment a fool gives up concentration and his other spiritual practices, he falls prey to fancies and desires." [90]

Although we already are the Absolute Reality, dedicated and sustained practice is required to remove the impurities (the kleśas and their resulting vāsanās/saṁskāras) that stand in its way.

Hence, yoga is a process of purification. Yoga sūtra 2.28 tells us:

"By dedicated practice of the various aspects of yoga impurities are destroyed: the crown of wisdom radiates in glory." [91]

And as we have seen in Part 1, the root cause of all impurities is ignorance (avidyā).

It is avidyā that results in the second affliction listed in yoga sūtra 2.3: the ego or I-thought (asmitā or ahaṁkāra) — the imposter self with its infinite number of special likes and hates that pretends to be the real you, thus covering up the real, infinite I-I (Brahman).

Swami Chinmayananda said of the imaginary or imposter self:

"All the Shastras and scriptures unanimously declare that our enemy is the ego. The sorrows and sighs belong to the ego–phantom. Sublimate the ego in constant vichar. In your discrimination of the real and the unreal, the false ego dream ends. End the ego and end the woes. If the ego in you is the samsarin**, if the ego in you is the tormentor, if the ego in you is the enemy, spy on him more closely and come to know who he is. Find out your enemy and drive him away.*

This ego, in fact, is a myth, a non-entity, a dream, a phantom, a mere false shadow. All the sorrows belong to this shadow of your own reality, and in your own thoughtlessness you have surrendered yourselves to the endless tyranny of this shadow. End the shadow for ever." [92]

*Enquiry
**One's mundane, worldly identity

The way to drive the ego away is simply to withdraw both our attention and belief in it. A total shift of reference point is required. Our identity must now become anchored in the Self or Seer.

In one of his talks, Swami Chidananda, a direct disciple of Swami Sivananda, expressed the degree of firm conviction required:

"Yes! Yes! Yes! That Timeless Being (Self) is the Reality and not this unreliable passing appearance. That nameless, formless, beginningless and endless Reality alone is real."

And with the understanding that the body and world are ephemeral. In the Aṣṭāvakra Gītā it is said:

"The body is nothing.
The world is nothing. When you understand this fully,
How can they be invented?
For the Self is pure awareness,
Nothing less". [93]

It is important, however, not to deny your experiences of the body or world. You are to lead a 'normal' life like everyone else. This includes looking after the health of the body, supporting your family, and having meaningful relationships.

Letting go of the belief in our false identity of body and mind is not an easy task, even though we are replacing it with something far superior. Be rest assured, however, that when one is endowed with unshakeable faith (in the teachings) and possessed with a strong desire for liberation, one is never left alone on this path. In addition to God within are unseen 'mighty companions' (described in the quote below), who are always by our side helping us along on our spiritual journey.

Swami Sivananda provides encouragement in the following quote:

"If you once make a strong determination and firm resolve, then it becomes very easy. You get interest and a new joy. Your heart expands and you have a broad outlook on life; you have a new wide vision. You feel the help from the invisible hands of the in-dweller of your heart. Your doubts are cleared by themselves, by getting the answer from within — you hear the still, sweet voice of God. There is an indescribable thrill of divine ecstasy from within. There is ineffable, unabating, undiminishing, undecaying spiritual bliss. This gives new strength and the footing on the path becomes firmer and firmer.

The jīvanmuktas (liberated sages), yogis, nityasiddhas (eternally perfect ones), amara-Puruṣas (immortal souls) and chiranjivas (deathless souls) lend their helping hands to the struggling aspirants. The aspirants feel this actually — the feeling of loneliness and of being neglected and forsaken vanishes entirely."

Once the mind is sufficiently purified through the various practices of yoga, knowledge of our true Self dawns, destroying ignorance once and for all. **Direct knowledge** of the Self is our true state and birthright. It is the pure beingness of asaṁprajñātā samādhi, also known as nirvikalpa samādhi, the eighth and final limb of yoga.

It should be highlighted here that asaṁprajñātā samādhi is not the goal of yoga — the goal is kaivalya or Self-realization. But it is by asaṁprajñātā samādhi that ignorance (the first kleśa and root cause of the other afflictions) is dispelled and the vāsanās (desires in subtle form) and saṁskāras (impressions/ imprints) become totally burnt in the fire of Knowledge, finally ending all possibility of re-birth.

In his introduction to his translation of Adi Śaṅkarācārya's Vivekacūḍāmaṇi, Śri Ramana Maharshi explains:

> *"Just as butter is made by churning the curds and fire by friction, so the natural and changeless state of Nirvikalpa [Asaṁprajñātā] samādhi is produced by unswerving vigilant concentration on the Self, ceaseless like the unbroken flow of oil. This readily and spontaneously yields that direct, immediate, unobstructed, and Universal perception of Brahman, which is at once **knowledge and experience** and which transcends time and space.*
>
> *This perception is Self-realisation. Achieving It cuts the knot of the Heart. The false delusions of ignorance, the vicious and age-long tendencies of the mind which constitute this knot are destroyed. All doubts are dispelled and the bondage of karma is severed."*

The importance of samādhi is also emphasized by Swami Vidyāraṇya, in several verses of Pañcadaśī. For example:

> *"By this samādhi, millions of actions accumulated in this beginningless world are destroyed and the pure inner qualifications (conducive to the Realisation of Truth) grow."*
> ~ Verse 1.59

> *"The experts in Yoga call this samādhi 'a rain cloud of dharma' because this samādhi showers the bliss of dharma in thousands of ways."* ~ Verse 1.60

> *"The web of vāsanās is totally destroyed and the hoard of actions known as merits and demerits is pulled out with its roots by this samādhi."* ~ Verse I.61

According to yoga sūtra 2.2, there are three acts of yoga without which significant spiritual progress and success in meditation (attainment of samādhi) are difficult. These are listed in yoga sūtra 2.1:

> *"Burning zeal in practice (tapas), self-study and study of scriptures (Svādhyāya), and surrender to God (Īśvara praṇidhāna) are the acts of yoga."* [94]

The three acts of yoga are examined further in Section 2 on the Niyamas (inner observances). We have also examined Svādhyāya extensively in Part 1.

Pause for Reflection

Reflect for a moment on your own special likes (rāga) and dislikes (dveṣa): your cravings or needs; and the things you hate or want to avoid. The greatest clue to identifying these is your emotions, which arise due to your innate tendencies/habits, often developed over many lifetimes. Notice when you experience excitement, hate, jealousy, guilt, selfishness, victimhood, pride, despair, and so on.

Practice and Detachment: The Two "Wings" of Yoga

In yoga sūtra 1.12, Patañjali tells us that for success in yoga, both practice (abhyāsa) and detachment (vairāgya) are necessary. These essentials are sometimes likened to the two wings of a bird.

In Part 1 you learnt through Self-enquiry (vichāra) to find that in truth you are Pure Consciousness (Ātman or Brahman). You used discrimination (viveka) to separate the 'Seer' from the 'seen'. Understanding the world to be but a false appearance helps loosen its hold on us. When we understand that everything is Brahman, our likes/attractions

> *"The abandonment of the illusory universe by realizing it as the all-conscious Ātman is the real renunciation honored by the great, since it is of the nature of immediate liberation."*
>
> ~ Aparokṣānubhūti (Verse 106)

(rāga) and aversions/hates (dveṣa) naturally begin to fall away. Then we begin to develop detachment or dispassion towards worldly objects (vairāgya).

The dispassion (vairāgya) required is towards the unreal. It is about giving up our false identification entirely. But simultaneously, it must be replaced by love or passion towards the real, the Self.

We love the Self or God by focusing the mind on it. This is practice (abhyāsa) — the steadfast centering in the Self, in both silent closed eye meditation and during daily activities.

Osho touched on this when he said:

*"The essence of abhyāsa is to be centered in oneself.
Whatsoever happens, you should not move immediately.
First, you should be centered in yourself, and from that
centering you should look around and then decide."*

And in yoga sūtra 1.14, we are told that our practice is to be done with the correct attitude. This is one of devotion, reverence and respect (satkāra).

As happiness is essentially our real nature, the practice of yoga and Self-enquiry slowly but surely leads us to a state of inner peace and quiet joy, even in what outwardly may seem to be difficult circumstances. This is a great blessing in life. We no longer need to take life so seriously when we understand it to be passing phenomena or Māyā (an appearance).

We also come to understand firsthand that vairāgya (detachment) is not about being outwardly cold or morose. We experience only more love and compassion to our fellow human beings when we understand them to be our very own Self. And we only have to look to accounts of the lives of jīvanmuktas (liberated sages) to see references to their wonderful sense of humor.

Eventually, for advaitic realization (final liberation), everything that is of an impermanent nature (composed of the 3-guṇas or qualities of nature), must be renounced or let go of. This is the subject of yoga sūtra 1.16:

> *"The ultimate renuniciation is when one transcends the qualities of nature and perceives the soul."* [95]

The last thing to be let go of is Īśvara (God in the dream of separation).

Method: Spying on the ego

Spying on the ego is watching how you react to others: 'listening in' as you judge or condemn someone, including yourself!

Observe when someone or something 'pushes your buttons', causing a negative reaction that disturbs your peace. Whenever you catch yourself reacting, know that it is the imposter self or ego and not the real you. Just watch and be the witness. Swami Venkatesananda, a direct disciple of Swami Sivananda, advised:

> *"Is it possible for you to look at someone with who you totally disagree and say, without hypocrisy, 'Sir, you may be right'? During those few moments watch what goes on within you. There is a combination of an earthquake, volcano, tornado and a tidal wave, all together. That is the ego. You've got it! Don't try to fix it. It hurts, it hurts. Good grief, it hurts. Watch what is happening inside you. That is the ego."* [96]

As the ego is not your real identity, do not believe what it says when it talks to you. Instead turn your attention towards that which is aware of the ego/thought. The Self, your true identity, looks on quietly but judges not.

This must be part of our practice of Self-enquiry (vichāra) — to catch (observe) the ego whenever it raises it head. As a result of this practice, the ego will slowly begin to fade away.

FIRST LIMB

YAMAS (Moral Restraints)

"Vedānta says, "O little man! Do not identify yourself with this perishable body. Give up 'I-ness' and 'mineness'! Do not hate your neighbor or brother. Do not try to exploit him as he is your own Self. There is a common Self or common consciousness in all. This is the same in a king and a peasant, in an ant and a dog, in a man and a woman, in a cobbler and a scavenger."
~ Swami Sivananda[97]

"And one of them, a lawyer, asked him a question to test him. 'Teacher, which is the great commandment in the Law?' And he said to him, 'You shall love the Lord your God with all your heart and with all your soul and with all your mind. This is the great and first commandment. And a second is like it: You shall love your neighbor as yourself. On these two commandments depend all the Law and the Prophets.'"
~ Matthew 22:35-40

THE first limb of yoga is the yamas or moral restraints. These are the moral codes that represent right or conscious living: how we engage with the world in everyday life, with our family, in the yoga community, and with colleagues and neighbors.

> *"One's spiritual realization lies in none other than how one walks among and interacts with one's fellow beings."*
>
> ~ B.K.S. Iyengar, *Light on Life*

When all is known to be Brahman, the practice of the yamas are naturally upheld. The yamas are: 1) non-violence; 2) truthfulness; 3) non-stealing; 4) energy preservation; and 5) non-coveting.

In Aparokṣānubhūti, Ādi Śaṅkarācārya described the Yamas as:

"The restraint of all the senses by means of such knowledge as 'All this is Brahman' is rightly called Yama which should be practiced again and again". ~ Verse 104

In this section, the yamas are presented from a perspective based on non-dual truth (that Reality is Para Brahman). Nonetheless, the insights and methods are meant to be practical so that you are able to incorporate them into everyday life.

How You See Others

I would like to share with you an important insight: Whatever you happen to think about another person, you are thinking that very same thought about yourself. At a deep subconscious level you know that there is only one of us. So, although it may seem that you are having thoughts about another person, at a subconscious level you interpret these thoughts as being about yourself.

Therefore, be very careful about what you think of others!

The way you should always view others, without exception, is as no less than Brahman, which is perfect love. You are then remembering what they really are. And by doing this you affirm to yourself that this is what you truly are. This gradually undoes the idea of separation in your subconscious mind.

A related warning: If you regard all you perceive with the five senses as an illusion and just stop there, this is how you will come to see yourself — also unreal! This results in feelings of emptiness and depression.

It is important, therefore, that you go all the way with your change of vision, replacing illusions with truth. It is only the names and forms that are illusory. The essence of everything, the Self or Brahman, is the underlying reality.

Seeing all and everything as Brahman is the fundamental

basis of the Yamas, and because of habitual thought patterns that make us see other people (and oneself) as separate bodies, we must remind ourselves of this fact again and again.

You now hold the key in which you are able to spiritualize life and your relationships – to actively see others as your very own Self or God, and to think and act accordingly.

This is the real practice of karma yoga – to serve others as no less than God. It is the mental attitude that is the most important. To quote Swami Sivananda:

"Why dost thou try to find God in deities and temples when thou has kept thy visible gods standing outside, hungry and naked? Regarding Him as manifest everywhere thou should serve all creatures with intense bhava [sentiment] if thou wishes to attain the highest perfection. Indeed, thy love towards the Lord should engender love for the whole universe for thou must see Him in all."

VISUALIZATION: **The Self in all beings**

Read the instructions once or twice and then proceed. The suggested time for this visualization is ten minutes or more.

Close your eyes and draw your attention to your Self. Be in your own presence for a few minutes.

Now bring to mind a person that you know. In order not to encounter too much resistance, begin with a person who does not trigger any negative emotions.

Using the power of your imagination, visualize your awareness as pure divine light expanding from your heart center until it completely encompasses both you and the other person.

Acknowledge that you both share the same one Pure Awareness. As this awareness or consciousness is omnipresent, there is no boundary where your awareness ends and that of the other person begins.

The final step is to visualize your respective forms (body and mind) falling away.

Only Pure Awareness remains.

Acknowledge that in truth, this person is your very own Self, not a separate person, no matter what the outer appearances may be.

This visualization can be done for a group of people such as family members, colleagues, or a larger group of people.

1) Ahiṃsā — Non-harming

"Condemn none; if you can stretch out a helping hand, do so. If you cannot, fold your hands, bless your brothers, and let them go their own way." ~ Swami Vivekananda

"And the King will answer them, 'Truly, I say to you, as you did it to one of the least of these my brothers, you did it to me." ~ Matthew 25:40

The basis for ahiṃsā (non-harming) rests on the fundamental principle of oneness. It is the belief in separation that causes all fear and negative emotions such as guilt, jealousy, anger and hate. We only harm others if we believe them to be separate entities.

Two of the ways that we can actively practice ahiṃsā are through kindness and forgiveness. In doing so we are cultivating the opposite virtues to that of harming.

You will come to see that the practice of kindness and forgiveness is different from the perspective of Advaita Vedānta than the way we traditionally practice these qualities.

Kindness

When we practice intrinsic kindness each and every day, we start to undo the idea that other people are separate from us. We begin to remember what they truly are. Being kind then becomes an expression of oneness. This is in comparison to the traditional type of kindness, which we offer with the expectation of something in return.

True kindness is based on the understanding that when we are unkind to others, we are hurting only ourselves. Attack, whether it be thought, verbal, or physical, is never justified because it is always based on the false premise that we are separate bodies. Unkindness, therefore, serves only to reinforce our wrong belief in separation thus binding us to the illusory world.

We must always offer kindness, even if we think the person does not deserve it, or if we never expect to see that person again.

Being kind is not only relevant to other humans, but to all living creatures.

If you find yourself being unkind, either in thought or action, immediately catch yourself and stop.

It is necessary to be vigilant for this, as our thoughts are a result of many lifetimes of mental conditioning. The practice of ahiṃsā, in all its aspects, therefore, requires a great deal of self-honesty and reflection.

Forgiveness

Before I describe true forgiveness, I would like to mention what it is not.

Briefly, forgiveness does not mean that we stand by and let someone physically assault us or allow oneself to be badly treated. We should always take necessary actions (such as leaving an abusive or exploitative relationship) to prevent others from doing harm, as necessary. Nor should we condone/make excuses for the unethical behavior towards others.

> *"Bless people when they revile you. Think how much good they are doing by helping to stamp out the false ego."*
>
> ~ Swami Vivekananda

Forgiveness is more of an inner practice, one based on the deeper spiritual truths that we have been examining up to now. As part of this practice, we should not deny our emotions caused by the suffering we have experienced.

With the above in mind, let us now examine true forgiveness.

Typically, when we practice forgiveness, we first judge someone to be guilty of doing something wrong and then make the decision to forgive them.

By comparison, true forgiveness is the deep recognition that whatever may appear to be happening, we are always at home in Brahman, dreaming of separation. It is the illusory cosmic mind, through the power of Māyā, that projected the world of names and forms. In truth, there is nobody 'out there' doing anything to us.

When we practice true forgiveness, we are remembering that the other person is not just a part of Brahman, but all of it. They have temporarily forgotten, however, what they are in truth.

True forgiveness is always carried out with God (Īśvara) or the Self, not with the ego. We do this is by being Self-attentive (abiding or resting in the Self) as we forgive.

Forgiveness is also based on our faith in the law of karma: that all suffering is a result of our own actions in this or a previous birth. As a result of this type of forgiveness, karma is burnt and vāsanās destroyed.

We have all come into our current life with a certain script which includes the lessons or karma that we have to work out (this is our prārabdha karma). This is usually centered around relationships, typically our family members (parents, siblings, partners, etc) and other significant people we meet in life. All the trials and tribulations we experience in life are God-given opportunities to undo the imposter self* by changing how we look at the world and others in it. In this way, our daily life becomes a classroom in which the mind is gradually healed.

*The constructed mind consisting of a bundle of vāsanās arising from beginningless ignorance and identification with being a separate body in countless lifetimes (see also Part 1, Chapter 13).

If we choose not to forgive, thus identifying with the ego's story of separation, Īśvara will present these lessons yet again, either in this or a future life.

True forgiveness is simple but not necessarily easy. There may be instances when we experience a great deal of resistance to forgiving others. Yet, without exception, we all reap the benefits of forgiveness. As we remove conflict from the mind, we will no long see conflict 'out there', in the dream of separation.

Forgiveness is required when anything occurs that results in lack of peace, whether it is an event we learn about from afar, something another individual has done or said to us, or a negative memory.

Depending on what needs to be forgiven, forgiveness is a process that may take time. For example, when we lose a loved one, we should not deny our emotions but allow ourselves to go through the grieving process. When we are ready to forgive our sense of loss, it should be a gentle process – a remembering of what the person truly is.

Ultimately, forgiveness is about not making things too real in the world of Māyā.

At times, however, it may seem that you are forgiving the same old thing again and again. This is where the quality of spiritual fortitude or forbearance (titikṣā) is important. This is the bearing of one's daily problems with cheerfulness or equanimity, in the spirit of true forgiveness.

However, this does not mean that you should resign yourself to fate. You should still take actions to improve a certain situation or difficulty that you find yourself in. At times, however, no matter how much we try, things simply do not go the way we had hoped.

Śri Sarada Devi refers to this in the following quote:

> *"Don't be afraid. Human birth is full of suffering and one has to endure everything patiently, taking the Name of God. None, not even God in human form can escape the sufferings of the body and mind"*
>
> ~ Śrī Sarada Devi [98]

"One suffers as a result of one's own actions. So, instead of blaming others for such sufferings, one should pray to the Lord and depending entirely on His grace, try to bear them patiently and with forbearance under all circumstances." [99]

Spiritual fortitude or forbearance (titikṣā) is a necessary qualification for Self-realization. Otherwise, any difficulties or obstacles we experience in life will detract us from spiritual practice.

Ādi Śaṅkarācārya explains:

"Those who are endowed with fortitude may attain the goal of yoga. Those who are not endowed with fortitude are overpowered by obstacles and they drift about like withered leaves before the wind". [100]

The following quotes from Guru Vachaka Kovai* are words of reassurance in the face of difficulties, which we will all experience at some point in life.

"The many afflictions which occur with severity like thunderbolts in the life of great devotees are only to establish their pure mind more and more firmly [in tapas, that is, Self-abidance] and not to shake them down [from it]."
~ Verse 617

"Discriminating and knowing well that all the sufferings that come by prārabdha in his life are sent to him by God's Grace in order to make his mind stronger and thereby save him, let an aspirant bear with them patiently as tapas without being alarmed even in the least." ~ Verse 618

"Just as a gem taken from a mine will not have full lustre if it is not polished on the grindstone, so the real tapas, the sādhanā which one is doing, will not shine well if it is not provided with trials and tribulations on its way." ~ Verse 619

"For a big temple-chariot to go along the streets and safely reach its destination, not only the strong linchpins but also the obstructing blocks, which prevent it from dashing into anything by running to the sides of the streets, are indispensable." ~ Verse 620

*The Garland of Guru's Sayings (Guru Vachaka Kovai) by Śri Muruganar is a comprehensive selection of Śri Ramana Maharshi's teachings.

2) **Satya — Truthfulness**

"God is truth, and He can be realized by observing truth in thought, word and deed." ~ Swami Sivananda

In his commentary to yoga sūtra 2.30, Śri Vyāsa defines truthfulness as when there is:

"speech and thought in conformity with what has been seen or inferred or heard on authority."

Related to truthfulness is honesty. Honesty is consistency between one's thought system and one's actual thoughts or actions.

What is our thought system now based on?

That the highest truth (Reality) is Pure Undifferentiated Consciousness or Perfect Oneness.

There are only two thought systems to choose from: that based on Oneness; or that of separation. The latter is the ego's thought system.

For significant spiritual progress, we should cultivate a constant awareness of the mind. It is only by doing so that we are able to apply discrimination as to whether we are upholding the right thought system.

On the need for this, Swami Sivananda advised:

"A man of discrimination is always careful, vigilant and circumspect. He always watches carefully his thoughts. He introspects.

He knows what is going on in his mental factory what Vṛtti [thought] or Guṇa [attribute or quality] is prevailing at a particular time. He never allows any evil thought to enter the gates of his mental factory. He at once nips them in the bud.

By his good thinking, by watching the nature of his thoughts, by introspection, by active noble thinking, the man of discrimination builds his noble character, forms his high destiny. He is careful in his speeches. He speaks little. He speaks sweet loving words. He never utters any kind of harsh words that can affect the feelings of others." [101]

The sole purpose of a human birth is Self-realization — waking up from the dream of separation. As Omniscient Inner Controller, only Īśvara knows what each of us needs to experience in order to realize the Self, as He/She has full knowledge of all our births — past, present and future.

Everything that happens in life does so for a reason in accordance with the law of cause and effect (law of karma). If something is meant to happen, there is nothing that we can do to prevent it.

Therefore, whenever we judge, resist or condemn a situation, we are no longer in alignment with this truth. We have withdrawn our trust in God and made the separation real. Similarly, when we condemn others or feel victimized, we are adhering to the wrong thought system – that based on separation.

The only course to take through the ups and downs of daily life is to be the silent witness (Sākṣī). Being the silent witness means watching your life from "above the battlefield" as it unfolds. It's as if you are watching a movie in which you are playing your part, yet at the same time knowing that it has nothing to do with your true identity. This allows life to unfold with grace, and in the most conducive way for Self-realization.

Remember!

It is important to take action and make decisions when needed. Applying discernment to situations is different from judgement, condemnation and resistance. How we act, mentally and physically, in each present moment determines what we will experience in the future. (See also Part 1, Chapter 13.)

Also, we should apply true forgiveness to any situation that results in a lack of peace.

Method: Self-enquiry and Satya (Truth/Honesty)

It is suggested that you carry out this method at regular intervals throughout the day, in the midst of whatever activity you happen to be engaged in. A minimum of five to ten minutes every hour is suggested in the beginning. As it is an internal exercise, it should not affect how you outwardly appear or behave.

Whenever you remember, be the silent witness and observe yourself as if you are an actor in a movie.

Behave as you normally do but inwardly witness your thoughts, emotions, spoken words, and physical actions.

Notice if your thoughts are not in alignment with the highest truth. A clue to this is seeing yourself condemning, judging, or getting irritated or angry. This is a sure sign that you have identified with your false identity (the body and mind) — the ego's thought system based on separation.

The next more subtle stage (again, to be applied during daily life) is to observe which of the gunas are prevailing in your mind at any given time. When the mind is agitated or restless with many thoughts and desires, usually of a self-centered nature, the quality of rajas predominates. Rajasic emotions include excitement, passion, anger, anxiety and jealousy. If you experience inertia, lethargy/sleepiness, or feelings of laziness, then tamas predominates. The mind is tamasic when there are the heavy emotional states such as boredom, depression, shame, apathy, and sadness.

Also, observe how the quality of your mind is directly affected by your practice of āsanas (yoga postures), prāṅāyāma (breathing exercises) and meditation. As rajas and tamas diminishes, the mind 'lake' becomes increasingly still and clear (sattvic) — without the large ripples of rajas or the muddying effect of tamas. A mind which is predominantly sattvic is one that is conducive to yoga and Self-enquiry. In such a mind there is discrimination, detachment, calmness, and happiness.

3) Asteya - Non-stealing

"Not knowing the power of flame, the insect falls into it.
The fish swallows the bait, not knowing the hook inside.
That, well aware of the vanity and dangers of the world,
We cannot give it up — Such is the power of Delusion."
~ Vairagya Shatakam (Verse 18)

> *"As long as a man has desires there is no end to his transmigration. It is the desires alone that make him take one body after another. There will be rebirth for a man if he has even the desire to eat a piece of candy."*
>
> ~ Śri Sarada Devi [102]

The root cause of stealing is want or desire. One way to actively practice asteya, therefore, is to lessen our cravings for worldly objects.

The following method provides a practical example of how Viveka (discrimination) and Vichāra (enquiry) may be used for dealing with cravings or desires immediately as they arise in the mind.

It is meant to be applied when you find yourself hankering after things in the world.

I would like to highlight here that it is the attachment to anything other than the Self that is the problem. It is not about physically giving anything up in the world. Common sense again is important here! It is okay to have goals in life and work towards these goals.

I have separated the process out into three steps: (i) Vichāra (enquiry); (ii) Viveka (discrimination); and (iii) Choose again.

With practice, however, the process becomes less segregated and more simultaneous as you learn to continuously witness your thoughts and apply a change of mind.

Method: Self-enquiry and Asteya (non-Stealing)

Vichāra (enquiry): When a desire or craving arises in your mind, investigate that which is aware of the desire — the Self. The desire is transient; it comes and goes in your awareness. You are not your desires!

Viveka (discrimination): Remind yourself that all desires (and thoughts) are of the false ego-mind drawing from the storehouse of past impressions (saṁskāras) and vāsanās (innate tendencies/desires in subtle form) from this and previous lifetimes. As the desired object or experience is impermanent, it ultimately results only in suffering. Only waking up to Absolute Reality (Brahman) can provide everlasting happiness. Nothing can be compared to the bliss of the Self.

Choose again: The part of the mind that is the decision maker (a function of the intellect), can choose to withdraw attention away from thoughts and desires. After having done so, remain as the Witness Consciousness.

Additional Note

Persistent desires can arise in the mind, generating a chain of thoughts and emotional pain caused by longing. Perhaps you think that your life would be so much better if only you came into the possession of a certain amount of money, a new job or partner, etc. In this instance too, vichāra (enquiry) is to be applied. Emotions are also objects of your awareness no matter how painful they may be. You are not your emotions!

It is best not to fight or bury painful emotions but acknowledge that they too will pass, even if it takes some time. Be gentle with yourself.

4) Brahmacharya — Energy Moderation

"You dissipate your desire for the Self by undertaking all kinds of useless activities that waste your time and lead to attachments. You think that your life is endless and that you can put off meditation till a later date. With this kind of attitude, you will die filled with regrets, not filled with peace."
~ Annamalai Swami Final Talks

"Tear your heart away from everything else; then seek God and you will surely find him." ~ Saint Teresa of Avila

The practice of Brahmacharya is to live for the quest of realizing Brahman — to find one's true happiness in this pursuit only. This is an inner discipline. It does not mean that we are to run away from our families, work or the world. We still must play our part scripted for us in our current life — whether it is as a householder or monastic.

The discipline of Brahmacharya is about not allowing our senses or mind to run loose due to the whole gamut of external objects and distractions. Lord Krishna tells Arjuna:

"The turbulent senses, O Arjuna, do violently carry the mind of a wise man though he be striving (to control them)."
~ Bhagavad Gītā (Verse 2.60)

With the observance of Brahmacharya, instead of letting our energies be dissipated outwards towards the various sense pleasures or objects, we harness and direct them towards spiritual practice. When focused in this way, they become a great motive force by which we are able to move towards our target, which is Reality itself. In the non-dual Reality there is no he, she, or desirable external objects.

In the following quote from *Yoga As A Universal Science*, Swami Krishnananda describes the state of affairs when we lack this observance.

> *"A lack of Brahmacharya means nothing but the presence of interests other than the interest in Yoga. The distracting object may be anything. If we have got a strong interest in something which distracts our attention, the energy goes. Any kind of leakage of energy in any direction, caused by any object or any event or context, is a break in Brahmacharya."*

More than any other yama, the practice of Brahmacharya (traditionally interpreted as celibacy) is dependent on both one's circumstances and stage in life. For example, it is not that God intends that we do not have children if this is part of our prārabdha karma.

But, whatever our circumstances, we can still examine how and where we invest our energy and question whether the choices we make in life will lead us closer or further away from Self-realization.

On the subject of desires, Śri Ramana Maharshi also made two important points that are worth reflecting upon.

First, sensory gratification only serves to magnify one's desires:

> *"Just as by (being fed with) ghee (clarified butter) a fire will only flare up and will not be calmed and extinguished, so by one's achieving and gratifying the desires one has formed, the fire of desire will never be satisfied and appeased."*
> ~ Guru Vachaka Kovai (Verse 592)

Second, once satisfied, a particular desire may seem trivial or pointless, compared to how we imagined. Yet, if we try to suppress it, the desire grows stronger until it becomes all-consuming.

"We have never seen any empty abyss that is so impossible to fill as intense desire, which can never be satisfied, because it (always) impoverishes one, making even an atom seem as great as Mount Meru before it is achieved, and vice versa after it is achieved." ~ Guru Vachaka Kovai (Verse 371)

Prior to Self-Realization, desires will arise in the mind as there are still vāsanās remaining. The way to remedy this situation is to abide in the Self.

As you begin to taste the bliss which is your very own nature, sensory gratification will become increasingly superfluous.

5) **Aparigraha** - Non-coveting

"Enveloped by the Lord must be This All — each thing that moves on earth. With that renounced, enjoy thyself. Covet no wealth of any man." ~ Iśā Upaniṣad (Verse 1)

Aparigraha, translated as non-grasping or non-coveting, is freedom from greed or wanting more.

In Part 1, I described how the world is a projection of the cosmic mind (Hiraṇyagarbha), through Māyā, onto the "screen" of consciousness, the underlying reality. This can be compared to a movie being projected onto a cinema screen; only the screen is real, remaining totally unaffected by the various scenes of the movie that appear on it.

Chasing after possessions or wealth in the world may perhaps be compared to watching a movie and trying to grab the illusory objects that appear on the movie screen!

We become further enmeshed in the world the more we run after it, as the very act of doing so creates further deep-seated vāsanās (innate tendencies/desires in subtle form). By lessening our desire for wealth or possessions, however, we make 'space' for divine presence (Ātman). This gives greater peace and joy compared to any object or experience available to us in the world of Māyā, and eventually leads to the highest bliss.

Method: Self-enquiry and aparigraha (non-coveting)

Whenever you find yourself coveting an object, possession, wealth, or aspect you think the world has to offer you, reflect:

This will not tempt me to delay my journey home to Perfect Oneness. Coveting this object only serves as a chain to bind me to this illusory world.

SECOND LIMB

NIYAMAS (Self-disciplines)

"The practice of the observances (Niyamas) is the highest bliss due to regular practice, by the wise, of oneness and rejection of the opposite (duality)". ~ Tejabindu Upaniṣad (Verse 18)

THE second limb of yoga is the niyamas, the self-disciplines or inner observances, consisting of: 1) purity; 2) contentment; 3) self-discipline; 4) Self-study; and 5) surrender to God (or Self). They result in a purified (sattvic) mind.

The aim of the niyamas is to become established in the knowledge of the unity of the Self with Brahman. They are, therefore, the very foundation of yoga or spiritual life.

Śri Ramana Maharshi defines niyamas in the following quote:

"This (Niyamas) is maintaining a stream of mental modes that relate to the Self and rejecting the contrary modes. In other words, it means love that arises uninterruptedly for the supreme Self." [103]

1) Śauca – Purity

"Those who, through holy grace, have purified their consciousness by remaining as the witness, will attain an awareness whose strength derives from its one pointedness. Through that awareness they will be freed from delusive desires and the terrors they bring, thus attaining the authentic state of supreme bliss free of all affliction."
~ Śri Muruganar, Sri Guru Ramana Prasadam

"Blessed are the pure in heart for they shall see God."
~ Matthew 5:8

Swami Sivananda describes both external and internal purity in the following quote:

"Purity is of two kinds, external and internal purity. External purity is cleansing of the physical body... Internal purity is cleansing of the mind of the dirt of attachment, hatred and other passions by the method of Pratipakṣa Bhāvanā, i.e., by cultivating the opposite virtues, and by the recognition of the evil in all objects of the senses." [105]

> *"The knowledge of one's identity with the pure Self that negates the wrong notion of the identity of the body as the Self sets a man free when it becomes as firm as the man's belief that he is a human being".*
>
> ~ Ādi Śaṅkarācārya[104]

The first step to gaining internal purity is to eradicate impure (rajasic and tamasic) thoughts, replacing them with pure (sattvic) ones. A method to achieve this, prescribed in yoga sūtra 2.33, is Pratipakṣa Bhāvanā: the cultivation of opposite virtues. For example, thoughts of jealousy are to be replaced by thoughts of happiness for the other person, thoughts of anger and irritation by forgiving thoughts, thoughts of hate with those of love, and so on. As a result, saṁskāras/vāsanās (imprints/ tendencies) that are opposed to the yamas and niyamas are replaced with 'yogic' (sattvic) ones and the afflictions (kleśas) are thereby weakened.

Lord Krishna describes one with a pure mind:

"He who hates no creature, who is friendly and compassionate to all, who is free from attachment and egoism, balanced in pleasure and pain, and forgiveness."
~ Bhagavad Gītā (Verse 12.13)

Eventually, even thoughts of a sattvic (pure) nature are to be thinned out. In Part 1 Chapter 13, I explained why, for Self-realization, vāsanās must be extinguished entirely. This is why the central aim of yoga is purification and control of the mind.

We do this by shifting the reference point of our identity, away from our thoughts or mind, to the Self. It is from here that we are to now engage with or act in the world. This automatically thins the vāsanās or thoughts (mind).

Depending on what activity you are engaged in, for example, focusing on a task at work, or practicing yoga āsanas, some thought is obviously required. However, the aim should always be to keep thoughts to a minimum and related to the task alone.

In the following quote Swami Sivananda provides advice on how to deal with unwanted thoughts:

"When all kinds of useless thoughts and emotions trouble you much, be indifferent (Udāsīna). Say to yourself: "Who am I?" Feel: "I am not the mind. I am the Ātman, the all pervading Spirit, śuddha Sacchidānanda. How can emotions affect me? I am Nirlipta, unattached; I am Sākṣī, witness of these emotions. Nothing can disturb me." When you repeat these suggestions of Vichāra or Vedāntic reflection, the thoughts and emotions will die by themselves." [106]

The following method provides further guidance on how to make the shift in identity to the Self. It is normal to lapse back into old thinking habits and ego identification. But with perseverance, transformation does happen. The mind becomes increasingly purified in direct proportion to effort, and such lapses become less and less frequent.

Even a small amount of progress is of tremendous help and benefit to spiritual life. Not only will you receive more inspired thoughts, but as the mind becomes predominantly sattvic you will become more cheerful, better able to concentrate, and possess great will power. All these qualifications are of paramount importance to realizing the Self. As a side benefit, they are also likely to bring success in worldly endeavors.

Most importantly:

When the mind (specifically the buddhi or intellect) is sufficiently pure, it is better able to reflect Brahman (the Original/ Pure Consciousness). This leads to success in Self-enquiry and meditation.

Yoga sūtra 2.41 tells us:

"When the body is cleansed, the mind purified and the senses controlled, joyful awareness needed to realize the inner self, also comes." [107]

Method: A Shift in Identity

Watch (witness) thoughts as they arise in the mind.

Notice whenever a thought appears that is unrelated to the activity you are engaged in.

Turn your attention to the Self (Witness) — that which is aware of thought.

Affirm to yourself:

I am that awareness that I feel right now. This is my true identity. The thought has nothing to do with my true nature.

Remain as the Witness no matter what activity you are engaged in.

If you forget and become entangled or emotionally involved in thought, do not despair or give up. As soon as you notice, become the Witness again.

Inspired Thought

Yoga sūtra 1.5, tells us that thoughts fall into two categories:
  (i)   painful/non-helpful (kliṣṭa); and
  (ii) non-painful/helpful (akliṣṭa).

Thoughts that are painful or non-helpful (kliṣṭā-vṛttis) are produced by the five kleśas (ignorance, egoism, likes, dislikes, and clinging to life). These thoughts, which are products of rajas and tamas, are detrimental to the practice of yoga. As they are based on the ego's thought system of separation, they include the 'loud' thoughts of judgement, condemnation, or victimization.

As the mind becomes more sattvic, however, inspired thought arises from the source of infinite wisdom within. Helpful thoughts (aklisṭa-vṛttis) are God-inspired thoughts. Their primary purpose is to gently awaken us from the dream of separation, and softly remind us what we are in truth. For example, you may get a flash of inspiration regarding a certain spiritual teaching resulting in greater clarity and understanding.

A clue that a thought is inspired is that it comes into the mind unbidden. There is also an inner sense of truthfulness, perhaps even a physical sensation such as a shiver up the spine, etc. Learning to tell the difference between inspired thought and ego-driven thought becomes part of the discrimination we are cultivating.

Inspired thought may also concern relatively mundane things. For example, an idea may pop up as to how to grow or manage your business, or you may experience an inner conviction about accepting a new job offer. Paradoxically, life tends to flow with greater ease as the mind develops greater purity.

This does not necessarily mean that things will always work out as one hopes. Whatever happens, the key is always to remember what you really are (the Self) and not to make the world of names and forms real.

2) Saṇtoṣa - Contentment

"There are four soldiers who guard the road to moksha (liberation). They are Patience (or peace of mind),

> **"Do not desire, for what you desire you get, and with it comes terrible bondage."**
>
> ~ Swami Vivekananda

Self-enquiry, Saṇtoṣa (Contentment), and Association with the Wise. If you can succeed in making one of these a friend, then the others will be easy. That one will introduce you to the other three." ~ Yoga-Vāsiṣṭha

Contentment is very important in spiritual life. Desires or cravings, of which there is no end, create further vāsanās. And in accordance with the law of cause and effect (law of karma), the right circumstances must then arise, in this or a future life, so that these latent desires may be realized.

In contrast, the practice of contentment leads to less striving and emotional resistance.

The fruit of contentment is a peaceful and tranquil mind that can now be fixed on the Self or God within. It is the Self alone that gives the highest bliss. Contentment, therefore, results in the highest happiness.

Of such a devotee, established in this niyama, Lord Krishna says:

> *"Ever content, steady in meditation, self-controlled, possessed*
> *of firm conviction, with the mind and intellect dedicated to*
> *Me, he, My devotee, is dear to Me."* ~ Bhagavad Gītā (Verse 12.14)

Pause for Reflection

Reflect for a moment on the transient nature of this short, fleeting life. We should not delay for an instant our efforts to realize the Self for the sake of the tiny pleasures of the world. This is the subject of the poem Vairagya Shatakam (the hundred verses of renunciation), from which the following verse is taken.

> *"Life is like a wave upon the waters,*
> *Youth only remains a few days.*
> *Wealth is like a fancy of the mind,*
> *It immediately vanishes.*
> *Enjoyment is like a flash of lightening*
> *Amongst dark clouds.*
> *Our most beloved one is only for a moment.*
> *Knowing this, O man, give your heart unto Brahman*
> *To cross this ocean of life."* ~ Verse 36

3) Tapas – Austerity

"By Truth can this Self be grasped, by Tapas, by Right Knowledge, and by a perpetually chaste life."
~ Muṇḍaka Upaniṣad (Verse III.i.5)

Yoga sūtra 2.43 tells us that tapas (austerity) is the self-imposed discipline which destroys all impurities.

The highest form of tapas is the continuous meditation on the Self, in both closed-eye (seated) meditation and during daily life as this requires intense self-discipline. We will be examining the methods for this in the later limbs of yoga.

Swami Sivananda explains:

> *"Only those supreme devotees who firmly stick to the remembrance of the Self as the foremost Sadhana are great tapasvins."*
>
> ~ Ramana Padamalai (Verse 116)

"True Tapas is meditation on the Self. It is fixing the mind on Brahman or the Self. It is to separate oneself from the physical body and the other four 'sheaths' and to identify oneself with the Absolute. It is to turn the mind towards the soul." [108]

Fixing the mind on the Self is the highest tapas because in doing so, we deny belief in the ego (ahaṁkāra) or imposter self — what we currently think of as 'I'.

As a result, grace befalls us. First in the form of deepening understanding (of the teachings). Then grace comes in the form of śraddhā — a firm conviction in both the goal of yoga and the means to the goal.

With śraddhā firmly established, a yearning for liberation begins to take hold. Our job is now to cultivate this desire for liberation as intensely as possible because Self-realization, or true life, is dependent upon it. This is the subject of the following quote by Śri Sadhu Om:

> **"Even as darkness disappears on turning towards light, ignorance disappears if you turn towards the light of the Self. As long as there does not arise a natural yearning for Self-knowledge, so long this ignorance or mental conditioning throws up an endless stream of world-appearance."**
>
> ~ Yoga-Vāsiṣṭha[109]

*"In order to qualify as an aspirant, one must have the absolute conviction that happiness, the sole aim of all living beings, can be obtained not from external objects but only from one's own innermost Self. When one has this qualification, an intense yearning will arise in one's heart to try to attend to and know Self. Indeed, for a true aspirant the desire and effort to know Self will become the most important part of his life, and all other things will be regarded as being only of secondary importance. **When such an intense yearning arises in one success is assured**, for where there is a will there is a way."*

~ The Path of Sri Ramana, Part 1

> **"One who is endowed with the strongest desire for liberation is liberated in this lifetime."**
>
> ~ Ādi Śaṅkarācārya [110]

The traditional Vedāntic analogy for the required intensity of this desire is that of a man being held under water. This is described by Swami Sivananda:

"Suppose you keep the head of a person immersed in water. He will be struggling for breath. He will intensely desire to get out of the water, so that he can breathe. Such intense desire for God-realisation is called Mumukṣutva."

~ Sadhana Chatustaya

Although this is a traditional analogy, we rarely pause to consider what this level of intense desire would actually mean in practice — if our head really was immersed in water. Michael

Langford, in his book *The Most Direct Means to Eternal Bliss* elaborates:

> *"He does not have time for discussion."*
> *"He does not have time for games."*
> *"He does not have time for endless reading."*
> *"He does not have time for television."*
> *"He does not have time for entertainment."*
> *"He does not have time for pretending to want to be free."*
> *"He does not have time for any dishonesty with himself."*
> *"He does not have time for pretending he has risen to*
>   *the surface."*
> *"He does not have time for debate or argument."*

Do not be put off! Most of us do not have this level of desire for liberation. The first step, however, is to recognize our degree of unreadiness, then choose to cultivate the desire for liberation at every opportunity.

On the need for honesty in this respect, Śri Nisargadatta Maharaj said:

> *"The desire to find the Self will be surely fulfilled, provided you want nothing else. But you must be honest with yourself and really want nothing else. If in the meantime you want many other things and are engaged in their pursuit, your main purpose may be delayed until you grow wiser and cease being torn between contradictory urges. Go within, without swerving, without ever looking outward."* ~ I AM THAT

Developing Self-Discipline

The first step in developing self-discipline is to establish a schedule for spiritual practice and then sticking to it at all cost. It is important, however, that you set yourself realistic goals.

As a minimum, the schedule should include what time you plan to wake up for meditation and how long to practice. It may also be helpful to set times for āsanas and prāṇayama.

It is also good to spend at least ten minutes for self-reflection each evening.

If you have work and family commitments which necessitate arising early for meditation, your planned schedule should also include what time you go to bed.

The benefit of preparing such a schedule is that it creates new life transforming habits. It will not be too long before you derive immense joy in relation to your spiritual practice and notice the positive impact it is having in all areas of your life.

Pause for Reflection

One way to increase the desire for liberation is to take a deep and honest, perhaps uncomfortable look at what Śri Nisargadatta Maharaj referred to as "the sorrow of the human state."

On this, Śri Nisargadatta Maharaj said:

"Until you realize the unsatisfactoriness of everything, its transiency and limitation, and collect your energies in one great longing, even the first step is not made." ~ I AM THAT

Perhaps you have experienced very few feelings of dissatisfaction or suffering in your life. Even so, you cannot avoid facing the unfortunate fact that the indefinite continuation of saṃsāra (cycle of birth and death) means that at some point, in a future lifetime, you will be subject to every possible kind of human suffering.

Anything you see or hear on the news, whether it is related to disease, natural disasters, acts of violence, wars, or atrocities are helpful reminders of all the possible types of human suffering that you will eventually experience if you continue to be born again and again.

As a means to increasing desire for liberation, it is also worth reflecting on the billions of cruel acts (both physical and verbal) that humans inflict on one another, including helpless children and animals, every day.

All that we see in the world is an outward manifestation of an inner condition. The inner condition of the ego-limited mind is born out of ignorance. All the evil and sorrow that arises does so due to our forgetting of who we truly are.

In the Yoga-Vāsiṣṭha it is said:

"The ego-sense is the source of endless sorrow, suffering and evil action." [111]

Cautionary Note!

As you observe the manifestation of the ego's thought system of separation, it is important not to make it real. You should see the world as an appearance only, no more real than when you watch a movie. This does not mean we should not be compassionate to the suffering of others and try and help when we can. A healthy (and appropriate) sense of humour is also a very helpful asset in spiritual life!

4) Svādhyāya - Self Study

"Knowledge is veiled in ignorance, and thereby mortals are deluded. But for those in whom this ignorance is destroyed by the Knowledge of the Self, that Knowledge, like the sun, reveals the Supreme. Fixing their minds in Him, at one with Him, abiding in Him, realizing Him alone as the Supreme Goal, they reach a state from which there is no return, their sins having been destroyed by their Knowledge."
~ Bhagavad Gītā (Verse 5.15-5.17)

Svādhyāya is the study or enquiry that leads to knowledge of the Self. In his commentary on the yoga sūtras, Ādi Śaṅkarācārya explains that this is the study of sacred texts (Upaniṣads) pertaining to release (liberation), in addition to repetition of the sacred syllable Om (also called the Praṇava).

Svādhyāya — Using the Sacred Syllable Om

The method of svādhyāya that we will first consider is reflection and meditation on the sacred syllable Om. The meaning of Om is the central subject of the Māṇḍūkya Upaniṣad, the shortest and yet most powerful Upaniṣad. Om is made up of three letters (a-u-m), but due to the rules of Sanskrit grammar, together they are pronounced as Om (as in home).

> *"The unreal world appears as real, whereas it is in reality a long dream arisen in our mind. As in dream, so in the waking state, the objects seen are unsubstantial, though the two conditions differ by the one being internal and subtle, and the other external, gross and long. This world is nothing but a long dream."*
>
> ~ Swami Sivananda[112]

In the next Self-enquiry exercise, you will examine your normal everyday experience, which consists of a continuous cycle of waking (jāgrad avasthā), dreaming (Svapna avasthā) and deep sleep (suṣupti avasthā). The constant factor present in each of the three states is the Self, the unchanging Witness.

In this method, the three letters of Om (a-u-m) are assigned to each of the three states.

The Self, the Pure Awareness underlying the three states, is designated by the silence after Om and is given the name Turīya, meaning the fourth. However, it is only the fourth in respect to the three (illusory) states. Turīya is the One Reality (Nirguṇa Brahman), and hence the only True Existence.

Self-Enquiry by Reflection and Meditation on Om

PART 1: REFLECTION ON THE MEANING

Slowly reflect on the description of the three states below, relating it to your own everyday experience.

Note: In the three states of waking, dreaming and deep sleep, consciousness appears to become identified with each of the three bodies: (i) Physical or gross body (Sthūla śarīra); (ii) Subtle body (Sūkṣma śarīra); and (iii) Causal body (Kāraṇa śarīra), respectively. (See descriptions on page 17.)

Waking (a)

During the waking state, you experience yourself to be an individual with a separate physical body and mind ('waker') in a physical universe ('waker's world').

Your waking life is made up of a continuous stream of successive experiences. Each experience consists of your awareness plus an object of perception (sight, sound, thought, etc).

All objects are transient and come and go (as a mental construct or vṛtti) in the light of your awareness.

The only permanent factor in the waking state is the Self which is consciousness or awareness.

Dreaming (u)

As you enter into the dream state, the physical senses (eyes, nose, ears, etc) no longer function.

As the dreamer, you experience a dreamer's body and dreamer's world which are mental in nature, produced from both the impressions of your waking experiences and latent desires.

The same awareness that witnesses objects in the waking state now witnesses dream objects.

The subject-object relationship in the waking state applies equally in the dream state. Swami Sivananda explains:

"In both states, waking and dreaming, objects are perceived, are associated with the subject-object relationship. This is the similarity between the two. The only difference between the two states is that the objects in dream are perceived in the space within the body, in waking they are seen in the space outside the body. The fact of their 'being seen' and their consequent illusoriness, are common to both states." [113]

Deep Sleep (m)

During deep sleep, neither the senses nor the mind function. The other two states of waking and dreaming exist in seed form.

In deep sleep there are no objects to be aware of and yet the Self (Pure Consciousness) remains constant, although seemingly enveloped in causal ignorance. In the Bṛhadāraṇyaka Upaniṣad, it is said of this state:

"That it does not see in that state is because, although seeing then, it does not see; for the vision of the witness can never be lost, because it is immortal. But there is not that second thing separate from it which it can see." ~ Verse IV.iii.23

Turīya (Silence)

When nescience (ignorance of our real nature as Pure Consciousness) is destroyed, the adjuncts to the Self, which are the gross, subtle, and causal bodies, are transcended. What remains is Turīya, the non-dual Brahman in which there is no-thing (no obect) to be seen.

Turīya is the unattached witness that shines in and through the states of waking, dreaming and deep sleep. It is the consciousness that illumines the silence that comes after Om each time you chant it.

As you reflect on the meaning of Om, and carryout the meditation described below, there should arise the intuitive understanding that the non-dual Turīya alone is permanent. This analysis is summarized by Ādi Śaṅkarācārya thusly:

"Objects of knowledge appear to exist in the intellect as
long as the intellect is there in the waking and dream states;
but none exists in the opposite case (i.e. when the intellect
is merged in deep sleep). The knower is always the knower.
Therefore, duality has no existence". ~ Upadeśa Sāhaśri
(Verse II.VII.5)

PART 2: MEDITATION BY REPETITION OF OM

For this practice, sit in a comfortable and relaxed position with the eyes closed. Begin chanting Om out loud on each out-breath. Then, when it feels right for you, continue with mental repetitions; 15 to 30 minutes is the suggested duration for this meditation.

As each Om falls into silence: Focus on the silence after each Om. 'Behind' this silence is Consciousness or Awareness — your true nature. It is the Awareness which underlies both the sound (chanting) of Om **and** the silence in between each Om.

Now proceed with mental chanting of Om. As you do so, identify yourself with the limitless ocean of Pure Consciousness in which the three states (waking, dreaming and deep sleep) appear to rise and fall like waves on the ocean.

Om from Īśvara's Perspective

In the previous method, you contemplated Om from the jiva's (individual's) perspective: Turīya (Ātman) associated with one body and mind.

You will now reflect and meditate on Om from Īśvara's perspective: Turīya associated with all beings.

At the cosmic level, the letters making up Om represent:

Letter	Name	Description	
A	Virāṭ	Consciousness (Seer) plus the entire physical universe (the cosmic physical body)	Saguṇa Brahman (Īśvara)
U	Hiraṇyagarbha	Consciousness (Seer) plus the subtle universe (the cosmic mind)	
M	Īśvara	**Higher** (parā) aspect: Consciousness (Seer) *plus* **Lower** (aparā) aspect: Material Cause - the causal universe (cosmic causal body)	
Silence	Brahman	Pure/Original Consciousness	Nirguṇa Brahman (Turīya)

By reflecting on the meaning of Om (see table above), you will begin to understand that it is truly everything — both Saguṇa Brahman (Īśvara) and Nirguṇa Brahman (Turīya).

In the next exercise, you will also discover that the letters a-u-m, when used to symbolize the physical, subtle and causal universe, do not stand for anything real (Sat) — but only an appearance in consciousness. By contemplating Om from the cosmic perspective, the universe is made to figuratively disappear back into Pure Consciousness.

First, a little more on Om:

The primal or first thought of creation appeared to arise in Brahman as a vibration or sound. This sound is Om, which happens to be the root of all sounds. It is from Om, therefore, that the names of all the objects manifested in the world are derived.

The world and its objects are materializations of the cosmic mind (Hiraṇyagarbha)* and depend on words for their expression. Therefore, both the object and the name (plus associated sound) used to signify it are ultimately non-different. And as all forms are illusory, their corresponding names and sounds are equally illusory. Hence, when an object is negated, the name and sound is also negated.

*In Part 1 Chapter 8, I described how the physical world is a projection of the cosmic mind though the power of Māyā.

Swami Nikhilananda, in his commentary to the Māṇḍūkya Upaniṣad further clarifies:

"...when Āuṁ is uttered, all the various parts of the vocal organ needed for uttering words are used. Therefore, Āuṁ is said to include all sounds. The substratum of all sounds is Āuṁ, and the substratum of phenomena is Brahman. The sounds signifying the phenomena are non-different from the phenomena, since both are illusory. When the illusion disappears, there remains only the substratum, which is one and admits of no difference. Therefore, it is said that Brahman is Āuṁ." [114]

Part 1: **Reflection on OM from Īśvara's Perspective**

Slowly reflect on each stage in turn:

Virāṭ (A)

Be aware of your own body or physical form.

As we examined in Part 1, awareness or consciousness (Seer) associated with all beings is Īśvara, the omnipresent Cosmic Seer (Draṣṭā).

As the physical universe is made up of matter/energy, everything in it is transient and ultimately unreal (mithyā).

Let the unreal physical universe drop away and the equally unreal A fall into silence.

Hiraṇyagarbha (U)

First be aware of your own mind — your thoughts, feelings and emotions that come and go. All are objects in your awareness.

As there is only one (cosmic) mind, acknowledge that the same one awareness encompasses all the seemingly fragmented minds.

All thought is matter/energy in subtle form and, therefore, unreal.

Let the unreal subtle universe drop away and the equally unreal U fall into silence.

Īśvara (M)

What remains after A and U have fallen into silence is consciousness (Seer) shining on no object at all.

As there can be no cause without an effect, M also falls into silence.

Brahman (Silence)

The Pure Consciousness that remains is the highest non-dual Reality.

Meditation on Om helps us to deeply assimilate the understanding that the Self (Pure Consciousness), in addition to being our internal Reality, is identical to the changeless substratum of all that appears to exist externally to us.

Initially, as we mentally repeat Om, we are to deeply reflect on its meaning. Hence thought is required. Eventually, however, (still repeating Om) we are to keep our attention on that which is beyond sound. The fruit of this meditation is samādhi (deep absorption).

> *"Initially the union with the higher should be established by concentrating on the sound (of Om). Then, one should meditate upon that Supreme that is beyond sound. By meditating on that which is beyond sound, the non-existence (illusory appearance of world) becomes existence (as the reality)."*
>
> ~ Amṛtabindu Upaniṣad (Verse 7)

Śri Ramana Maharshi explains:

"The purport of prescribing meditation on the Praṇava is this. The Praṇava is Oṃkāra… the advaita-mantra which is the essence of all mantras…. In order to get at this true significance, one should meditate on the Praṇava. …The fruition of this process is samādhi which yields release [mokṣa], which is the state of unsurpassable bliss." [115]

PART 2: **MEDITATION**

Transcending the Universe Using Om

As in the previous meditation, you may wish to begin chanting Om out loud for some minutes (using the correct pronunciation: Om as in home) and then continue with mental repetitions.

On each repetition of Om (see also hints below):

O: Merge (see hint 1) the gross world (your own body plus the entire physical world) into the subtle world (your individual mind along with the cosmic mind).

M: Merge the subtle world into the causal world (thoughts in seed form).

Silence: Merge the causal world into the Ātman.

In the silence after each Om:

Shift your attention from the silence to the consciousness that is aware of the silence.

As the silence becomes 'deeper', the consciousness will become increasingly evident.

At some point it may feel natural to allow the repetition of Om to drop off altogether. Although it may be re-introduced at any time during the meditation, for example, if thought agitations begin to arise.

And then?

There is nothing that remains to be done except attend to the subject (consciousness).

Identify with the subject.

Eventually even the silence will disappear and become absorbed in You, the Pure Consciousness.

Hints:

1. In the instructions given above: to 'merge' means to transcend. Each time you repeat Om, you are to completely withdraw your attention away from the physical body (plus objective physical universe) and all thought activity, and turn it inwards, towards the background of awareness or consciousness (the subject).

2. This meditation provides the mind with an object of support (in this case, the sound symbol Om) for practitioners who initially find meditation without support (introduced in Part 1, chapter 5) difficult.

3. If you have been initiated into a mantra, this meditation method may still be used, but with your chosen mantra in place of Om. The mantra is a sound symbol for God with a particular name and form. The silence after each mantra symbolizes God without form. As you repeat the mantra, therefore, allow the form aspect to be transcended

and focus on the silence after each repetition as described above.

4. The four main obstacles that come up during meditation and practical suggestions on how to manage them are discussed at the end of the seventh limb.

The aspect of svādhyāya we will now consider is the study of scriptures. For yogis this typically includes both the yoga sūtras, and scriptures such as the Bhagavad Gītā and the Upaniṣads. The Bhagavad Gītā is often described as being the very essence of the Upaniṣads.

> *"That which is the finest Essence — this whole world has that as its soul. That is the Reality. That is the Ātman.*
>
> *That thou Art".*
>
> ~ Chāndogya Upaniṣad (Verse VI.14.3)

Scriptures point us to the goal of spiritual practice and tell us of the nature of Brahman or Reality. Hence the necessity to include this aspect of svādhyāya in our spiritual practice.

In the following quote, Śri Sarada Devi tells us the real purpose of studying scriptures, and simultaneously provides us with a warning:

> *"Does one get faith by mere studying of books? Too much reading creates confusion. The Master [Śri Ramakrishna] used to say that one should learn from the scriptures that God alone is real and the world illusory."* [116]

As our mind becomes increasingly purified and we surrender ourselves to God or the Self (the subject of the next niyama), our understanding of the scriptures becomes deeper. Reading the scriptures then becomes more of a meditation — a time spent in deep contemplation.

The Mahāvākyas are the great sayings of the Upaniṣads which establish identity or oneness of the Self (Ātman) with Brahman.

Deep contemplation on the Mahāvākyas provides us with a means of Self Study (svādhyāya) based on the scriptures.

The four principal Mahāvākyas are:

Prajñānam brahma (Consciousness is Brahman) ~ Aitareya Upaniṣad

Ayam ātmā brahma (This Self is Brahman) ~ Māṇḍūkya Upaniṣad

Tat tvam asi (That Thou Art) ~ Chāndogya Upaniṣad

Aham brahmāsmi (I am Brahman) ~ Bṛhadāraṇyaka Upaniṣad

We will now look at two of these Mahāvākyas in more detail followed by a contemplation exercise.

> **"Those who do not dive into the Heart**
>
> **And confront the Self in the five sheaths hid**
>
> **Are only students answering out of books**
>
> **Clever questions raised by books,**
>
> **And not true seekers of the Self."**
>
> ~ Guru Vachaka Kovai (Verse 592)

Prajñānam brahma — Consciousness is Brahman

Swami Vidyāraṇya, in Pañcadaśī, defines the meaning of 'Prajñānam' as:

> *"That by which a man sees, hears, smells, speaks and distinguishes sweet and bitter tastes etc., is called consciousness."* ~ Verse V.1

This Mahāvākya tells us to identify the I AM or background of awareness (witness consciousness) that we feel *right now* to be no other than Brahman (Pure Consciousness) as it has no independent reality other than That.

The example given in Part 1 Chapter 10 was the reflected light from the moon which we know to originate from the sun (original light).

We also examined how the I AM is reflected consciousness (cidābhāsa) — the effect of the Pure/Original Consciousness being reflected in the mind. The I AM is the witness (observer) of the mind and intellect.

Śri Ramana Maharshi explains:

"If, without meditating on that as being identical with oneself, one imagines it to be different, ignorance will not leave. Hence the identity meditation is prescribed." [117]

Similarly, in his text Upadeśa Sāhaśri ('A Thousand Teachings'), Ādi Śaṅkarācārya writes:

"As one cannot become another, one should not consider Brahman to be different from oneself. For if one becomes another one is sure to be destroyed." ~ Verse II.XV.1

And underneath this verse, Ādi Śaṅkarācārya adds the following clarification:

"The idea is this: The individual Self, if considered to be really different from Brahman, cannot become Brahman as long as it exists; and if it were destroyed who would then become Brahman? Therefore one should know that one is not different from It and It is not different from one."

Tat tvam asi — That Thou Art

In this Mahāvākya, 'Tat' (That) refers to Brahman. This is described by Swami Vidyāraṇya in Pañcadaśī:

"Before the creation there existed the Reality, one only, without a second and without name and form. That is even now (after creation) exists in a similar condition is indicated by the word 'That.'" ~ Verse V.5

Tvam (thou) is referring to the inner Self which is of the nature of Pure Consciousness. The Mahāvākya 'Tat tvam asi' therefore asserts their identity. Swami Vidyāraṇya explains:

"The principle of consciousness which transcends the body, senses and mind of the enquirer is here denoted by the word

*'thou'. The word 'Asi' (art) shows their identity. **That identity has to be experienced.**"* ~ Pañcadaśī (Verse V.6)

A Simple Contemplation Exercise on the Mahāvākyas

Read the instructions once or twice and then proceed.

Close your eyes and turn your focus inward towards your awareness or inner Presence (I AM).

Reflect on the fact that this very awareness is Pure Consciousness (Brahman) reflected in the mind.

Using the power of your imagination, visualize Pure Consciousness as divine light shining through your mind. Feel engulfed by this divine pristine light.

Allow the mind, which is inert and made of subtle matter, to fade away.

You, the limitless Pure Consciousness remains.

Deeply contemplate as you rest in your awareness:

I *am that Infinite Pure Consciousness.*

and

I AM Brahman.

Now drop all mental constructs — even the Mahāvākyas.

Just Be.

Note!

The Mahāvākyas are not meant to be repeated mentally like a mantra but are to be used only as a pointer to the truth within you.

5) **Īśvara Praṇidhāna** — Surrender to God

"Surrender to Him and abide by His will whether he appears or vanishes; await His pleasure.

If you ask Him to do as you please, it is not surrender but command to Him. You cannot have Him obey you and yet think that you have surrendered. He knows what is best and when and how to do it. Leave everything to Him; His is the burden, you no longer have any cares. All your cares are His. Such is surrender. This is bhakti". ~ Śri Ramana Maharshi (Talks, 450)

In this section, we will be looking at how you may put Īśvara Praṇidhāna (surrender to God) into practice in everyday life, the result of which is grace. B.K.S. Iyengar tells us:

> *"Through surrender the aspirant's ego is effaced, and the grace of the Lord pours down upon him like torrential rain."* [118]

> *"In Īśvara Praṇidhāna (surrender to God) you are required to completely get rid of your present wrong consciousness based upon the outer context of the temporary phenomenal environment and to develop within you a consciousness where you know of yourself in relation to the Eternal."*
>
> ~ Swami Sivananda

It is by the Lord's grace that we gain the capacity to understand the path of yoga, in addition to finding ourselves in the right circumstances for spiritual practice.

When we surrender, God removes all obstacles (physical, mental and spiritual) to Self-realization. As a result of grace, kleśas (afflictions) are weakened, vāsanās become exhausted and karma undone, as God leads us gently and surely home to Perfect Oneness.

Hence, we can understand why Śri Sarada Devi advised her devotees:

> *"The grace of God is the thing that is needful. One should pray for the grace of God."* [119]

To gain the grace of God and therefore more easily attain samādhi, Patañjali prescribed meditation on Īśvara using the sacred mantra Om*. Not as mere mechanical repetition but accompanied with reverence (feeling) and understanding of its meaning (significance). For example in yoga sūtras (1.28-1.29) it is said:

"The mantra āuṁ [om] is to be repeated constantly, with feeling, realizing its full significance."

"Meditation on God with the repetition of āuṁ [om] removes obstacles to the mastery of the inner self." [120]

*See Meditation: Transcending the Universe Using Om on page 160.

The repetition of Om also helps us to remember God (and be Self-attentive) during daily life, not just in seated meditation. Śri Ramana Maharshi explains:

"He who gives himself up to the Self that is God is the most excellent devotee. Giving one's self up to God means remaining constantly in the Self without giving room for the rise of any thoughts other than that of the Self." [121]

How do we do this practically? We still must act in the world and perform our functions and duties in life. But as soon as the mind is freed up and we remember, for example, as we perform routine tasks, we are to mentally repeat Om (or your personal mantra if you have been initiated into a mantra).

We have already examined the meaning of Om earlier in the section on Svādhyāya (Self Study). In the following quote, Swami Sivananda reminds us of its great significance:

"Om (Aum) is everything. Om is the Name or symbol of God, Īśvara, Brahman. Om is your real name. Om covers the whole threefold experience of man. Om stands for all the phenomenal worlds. From Om this sense-universe has been projected. The world exists in Om and dissolves in Om. 'A' represents the physical plane, 'U' represents the mental and astral plane, the world of intelligent spirits, all heavens. 'M' represents the whole deep sleep state, and all that is unknown even in your*

wakeful state, all that is beyond the reach of the intellect. Om represents all. Om is the basis of your life, thought and intelligence. Om is everything. All words which denote objects are centered in Om. Hence the world has come out of Om, rests in Om, and dissolves in Om." [122]

*Waking, dreaming and deep sleep.

The following meditation is a variation of the one given earlier (on page 160). It is a matter of personal preference, but you may find this next method to be particularly helpful for times other than seated (closed eye) meditation, for example, during a walk.

> **"He who utters Om with the intention 'I shall attain Brahman' does verily attain Brahman."**
>
> ~ Taittirīya Upaniṣad (I.viii.1)

You may also wish to experiment with repeating Om on each breath in the following manner: 'o' on the in-breath, and 'm' on the out-breath. As you repeat Om, try to feel that it arises out of You.

Method: Īśvara Praṇidhāna Using Om

In this method, the three letters of om (a-u-m) are used to symbolise Īśvara as the Creator, Maintainer, and Destroyer of the world, respectively.

The silence that comes after each Om represents Para Brahman, the substratum of Reality behind all names and forms.

As you proceed with the mental chanting of Om, simulate in your mind Īśvara's infinite cycles of creation, maintenance and destruction. All this arises in You, the Pure Consciousness that remains completely unattached and untouched.

Begin to cultivate Brahma-Bhāvanā: Feel that your own awareness or consciousness has no independent reality from the Infinite Pure Consciousness. As you abide in the Self, know that this Consciousness is all there is — the only Reality — an

Infinite Ocean of Light. Feel that the entire universe, the creation of Īśvara, is like a straw floating in You the Infinite Ocean of Consciousness.

To know Brahman is to become Brahman. The reason is expressed simply by Swami Krishnananda in his commentary on The Moksha Gita by Swami Sivananda:

"Whatever one thinks, that he becomes, for the source of imagination is the omnipotent Self."

Handing Over All One's Burdens and Attachments to God

The practice of Īśvara Praṇidhāna is the acknowledgement that God is omniscient (all-knowing) and therefore knows what is best for us, at each step of the way, to reach the goal of liberation. Now, with firm faith, we understand our life to be unfolding exactly how it is meant to.

As the knowledge of our oneness with God becomes deeply assimilated and the belief that we are a separate individual attenuated, our intuition (and trust in it) grows increasingly stronger. It is with both relief and a strong sense of gratitude when we come to the firm conviction that: Yes! I can handover all my decisions to God by resting in the Self and allowing guidance (as inspired thought) to come from here, the center or ground of my own being.

In the following quote, Śri Ramana Maharshi tells us that all of our cares and concerns, which include our attachments, are to be handed over to God.

"Whatever burdens are thrown on God, He bears them.
Since the supreme power of God makes all things move,
why should we, without submitting ourselves to it, constantly worry ourselves with thoughts as to what should be done and how, and what should not be done and how not? We know that the train carries all loads, so after getting on it why should we carry our small luggage on our head to our

discomfort, instead of putting it down in the train and feeling at ease?" [123]

Although it is okay to have certain preferences regarding what is to transpire in one's life; we must be prepared not to be attached to the outcome. Only Īśvara (God) has the full picture and knows what is best for all concerned. This is the subject of the following quote by Śrī Ramana Maharshi:

"If you have surrendered, you must be able to abide by the will of God and not make a grievance out of what may not please you." ~ Talks with Śrī Ramana Maharshi (Talks, 43)

When we abide in the actionless Self, we still perform the duties or actions that are required of us. Internally, however, we are to feel that it is nature, by the Will of God, that does everything.

Swami Sivananda clarifies this in the following quote:

"It is the idea of agency, the idea I am the doer that binds man to Saṃsāra. If this idea vanishes, action is no action at all. It will not bind one to Saṃsāra. This is inaction in action. If you stand as a spectator or silent witness of Nature's activities, feeling Nature does everything; I am non-doer (Akarta), if you identify yourself with the actionless Self, no matter what work or how much of it is done, action is no action at all. This is inaction in action. By such a practice and feeling action loses its binding nature." [124]

All actions are to be performed without any selfish motive or desire for reward, but as an offering to God. Then we are no longer bound by the law of karma.

Lord Krishna tells us:

"Whatever thou doest, whatever thou eatest, whatever thou offerest in sacrifice, whatever thou givest, whatever thou practice as austerity, O Arjuna, do it as an offering unto Me."
~ Bhagavad Gītā (Verse 9.27)

Pause for Reflection – Being in the world but not of it

When a householder devotee asked the great saint Śri Ramakrishna*, "How ought we to live in the world?" he replied:

"Do all your duties, but keep your mind on God. Live with all, with wife and children, father and mother and serve them. Treat them as if they were very dear to you, but know in your heart of hearts that they do not belong to you."
*From *The Five Commandments of Sri Ramakrishna* by Swami Dayatmananda

The example that Śri Ramakrishna gave was that of a maid servant in a rich man's household. The maid servant serves, loves and cares for the household she is with, but all the time her mind is focused on where she truly belongs: with her family back in her home village.

We too are to play our part in life, being a good and loving parent or spouse, etc. At the same time, we must understand that attachments to others at the level of form results only in bondage.

In an article printed in the Vedānta Magazine, where he discusses Śri Ramakrishna's advice to householders, Swami Dayātmananda explained:

"No one really belongs to anyone in this world. A Sanskrit poem says: Just as twigs being carried by the current in a river come nearer and again get separated so also people come nearer and get separated according to the results of their past actions. This is absolutely true. If we look back into our past we can realize how true this statement is. The One and only Eternal Companion of our life is God alone. We learn this truth only after much suffering. Every being in this world is journeying towards God, the final destination of all. The journey comes to an end only when we reach Him. Therefore all the unions and separations in this world are

only accidental and meant only to help us develop detachment and devotion. Until we learn our lessons we will be presented with the same situations and difficulties."

Prayer

Prayer is most helpful in spiritual life. It is a means by which we develop love for the divine.

The best prayer we can make to God, with reverence and gratitude, is that:

He/She be in charge — that God's will alone is our will.

> *"Pray to God with tears in your eyes whenever you want illumination or find yourself faced with any doubt or difficulty. The Lord will remove all your impurities, assuage your mental anguish, and give you enlightenment.."*
>
> ~ Śri Sarada Devi[125]

We ever remember Him/Her.

We see the world differently, which is to make it all the same (Brahman).

We develop all the necessary qualifications for Self-realization including the burning desire for liberation.

He/She removes our ignorance by helping us to remember that our only ever problem lies in our belief in separation.

That He/She removes the obstacles in meditation such as negative thoughts, mental agitation, etc.

Related to the subject of prayer:

We should understand that Īśvara corrects the mind at the level of *cause* which is the Kāraṇa Sarīra (Causal Body) — the seat of the vāsanās/karma; and not at the (gross or physical) level of form or world appearance — the *effect*.

Using the analogy of a movie, if we want to change something that is appearing on the movie screen we would naturally have to turn around, find the hidden projector and change what is in it. What happens on the screen will then automatically change.

When we pray to God for help, therefore, we should ask for help at the level of cause. Asking for things at the level of effect (world appearance) is a demand on God, not surrender.

True prayer is silence — the silence in which we abide in the Self. Through the practice of surrender or abiding in the Self, Īśvara's correction is automatically invited. But this may or may not be experienced as a change in our external circumstances. Be assured, however, that change does take place (vāsanās get destroyed and karma burnt) at a sub-conscious level even if we are not consciously aware of it.

THIRD LIMB

ĀSANAS (Seat/Postures)

*"We are missing the gold if we do āsanas
as a physical practice only."*
~ Geeta S. Iyengar

THE practice of yoga postures (āsanas) provides us with an unequalled means for maintaining the physical health of the body and making it strong and fit for seated meditation. Not only that, a gradual transformation of the mind takes place. As you practice yoga, you can

> *"Man is bound when he identifies himself with Nature and its effects — body, mind, Prāṇa or the life-force, and senses. He attains mokṣa when he identifies himself with the immortal, 'actionless' Self that dwells within his heart."*
>
> ~ Swami Sivananda[126]

and should, observe the effect it has on your mind.

In one of his talks* Swami Chidananda explained the subtle shift in the quality of the mind that takes place. Initially there is an increase of rajas-guṇa, the tamas-guṇa becoming secondary. Finally, rajas-guṇa becomes controlled and sattva-guṇa predominates. This helps to prepare the mind for the higher limbs of yoga. Swami Chidananda continues:

> *"This change in the Triguṇa proportion and the augmenting of the Sattva-Guṇa has its effect on the mind. The heart becomes purified, the mind becomes Sattvic and subtle, and*

thoughts become pure. Thus Haṭha-Yoga effectively enables the seeker to gradually gain remote control over the mind.

By themselves they [āsanas, prāṇāyāma, etc] do not have the power to attain God-realisation, but they help us in indirect ways. They bring about within our mind, thoughts, feelings, and our very consciousness ultimately a gradual transformation. And when that transformation becomes complete, then our entire being becomes prepared for receiving God's grace. They are a preparation."

*Recorded in Prerequisites for Knowledge, published by the Divine Life Society.

We can greatly help this process of transformation by the way we approach our yoga practice. In the disciple/guru dialogue in Swami Sivananda's book Vedānta for Beginners, the disciple asks:

"How can I transcend the three bodies?"*

*our body-mind complex made up of the three bodies (gross, subtle and causal) or five sheaths.

The Guru answers:

"Identify yourself with the All-pervading, Eternal Ātman. Stand as a witness (Sākṣī) of all experiences. Know that the Ātman is always like a king – distinct from the body, organs, vital breaths, mind, intellect, ego and Prakṛti — the Witness of their attributes." [127]

Herein lies the key with which we should practice yoga āsanas or postures:

We spiritualize our āsana practice by practicing with the Self, instead of the ego. It then becomes a form of Self-enquiry or meditation, no longer a purely physical practice.

The following method provides a starting point for developing such a practice with the Self.

Self-enquiry and the Practice of Yoga Postures (Āsanas)

The suggested entry point for becoming the Witness (Sākṣī) during your āsana practice is the breath. As soon as you notice that you have gotten lost in thought, simply begin again by bringing the focus back to the breath.

The following guidelines are not meant to be taken as a prescriptive method but rather to provide some hints as to how one is able to stand as the Witness of the five sheaths – the 'Watcher from the inside'. For convenience, the sheaths are presented from the outside in.

Annamaya kośa
(Food stuff sheath)
Observe the various parts of your physical body as you move into and hold each posture.

> *"You watch yourself from inside. It is full of silence."*
>
> ~ B.K.S. Iyengar, *Light on Life*

Observe the shape that your physical body makes in space.

Prāṇamaya kośa (Vital (life) force or energy sheath)
Observe your breath. Notice its rhythm.

Scan and observe your physical body from the inside. Be aware of your internal life force. Feel the life force in your hands, feet, everywhere you can. Observe feeling hungry, tired or energetic.

Manomaya kośa (Mind sheath)
Witness thoughts as they arise in the mind. In order to keep the mind quiet, however, try not to engage with thought that is not related to your practice. Observe if the emotional state of your mind changes.

Vijñānmaya kośa (Intellect sheath)
Observe as you make decisions with regard to your practice, for example: physical adjustments in the various postures, sequencing of postures, etc.

Ānandamaya kośa (Bliss sheath)
As your mind becomes steadily transformed by your yoga practice, a sense of inner sattvic joy may arise — a deep sense

of well-being. This joy has 'trickled down' from the Bliss Sheath. Observe this.

Ātman

Once settled in a certain yoga posture, turn your focus to your awareness — your quiet center.

Be aware of your awareness.

Watch the Watcher.

Abhiniveśa and the Practice of Yoga Postures

Abhiniveśa is the clinging to life or fear of death. In yoga sūtra 2.9 this is described as the subtlest of all the afflictions and one which is "found even in wise men." [128]

Identification with the body results only in suffering and re-birth. We should, therefore, eliminate this idea at all costs, particularly in relation to our āsana practice. We should not allow the practice of yoga postures to increase our attachment to the body and make it even more real.

Ādi Śaṅkarācārya also gave the following warning:

"He who seeks to know himself while pampering the body is a crossing a river holding onto a crocodile in mistake for a log." ~ Vivekacūḍāmaṇi (Verse 84)

As mentioned earlier, it is important to look after the body. And yet physical problems such as those due to injury, accidents, diseases, will at some point be experienced by all of us, in varying degrees, regardless of how many yoga postures we have been able to master. Physical problems should always be seen as an inconvenience only and nothing more. Our true identity is beyond any kind of physical suffering.

Ultimately our āsana practice provides us with an opportunity to look deeply at what the body is: a series of sheaths made-up of inert matter that veil our real nature. We can then disidentify with it, just as we disidentify with the bodies we appear to take on in dreams after waking up.

On this, Ādi Śaṅkarācārya said:

"Just as you have no self-identification with your shadow-body, reflection body, dream body or imagination body, so you should not have with the living body either."
~ Vivekacūḍāmaṇi (Verse 163)

In this section, I have attempted to describe how you may spiritualize the practice of haṭha yoga postures so that it becomes a means of meditation and Self-enquiry.

By the term āsana, however, Patañjali was referring specifically to the various sitting postures used for meditation. I mention this to emphasize that the practice of yoga postures that enables you to sit comfortably for an extended period is very helpful for your practice of seated meditation (seventh limb of yoga). During seated meditation there is to be as little body consciousness as possible.

> **"Yoga is completely an inward process, for it is not the body that is the hindrance to Absolute Independence but the mind.**
>
> **Any physical practice done to achieve Spiritual Perfection should be coupled with inward detachment and love for the Eternal." "**
>
> ~ Swami Krishnananda[129]

Swami Sivananda further explains:

"In Patañjali's Yoga, Āsana does not mean a specific posture, but means sitting. It means, mainly, sitting for meditation. Āsana means a meditative seat. The way in which you sit for meditation should be such that the body is motionless and steady, and also, it should not cause any discomfort to the body; otherwise, it cannot be maintained for a long time. It is only when the posture is comfortable that you can maintain it for a long time. Maintaining the Āsana for a long time is of paramount importance to facilitate proper meditation. The whole science of Yoga is only to prepare the person for

meditation physically, vitally and mentally. So, a comfortable posture is a very important thing. The factor of comfort is very important. This is emphasized by the very terse definition of "Āsana" in Patañjali's Yoga, namely, "Sthira Sukham Āsanam".*

    *The yoga sūtra quoted is 2.46: Sthira means firm, fixed and lasting; and Sukham is happiness.

It is for this reason, that a chair may be used for meditation purposes — but only if necessitated by age or physical limitations.

FOURTH LIMB

PRĀṆĀYĀMA
(Control of Vital Energy)

*"As breath stills our mind, our energies
are free to unhook from the senses and bend inward."*
~ B.K.S Iyengar, *Light on Life*

PRĀṆĀYĀMA is even more effective than yoga postures at transforming the nature of the mind. In yoga sūtra 2.52 it is said:

> *"Prāṇāyāma removes the veil covering the light of knowledge and heralds the dawn of wisdom."* [130]

This 'veil' is rajas and tamas. In his book Raja Yoga, Swami Sivananda explains:

> *"When you feel present yet formless, do you not feel an absence of specific identity?*
>
> *You are there, but who is there? No one.*
>
> *Only present Awareness without movement and time is there.*
>
> *Present Awareness is the disappearance of time in human consciousness."*
>
> ~ B.K.S Iyengar, *Light on Life*

"By the practice of Prāṇāyāma, Rajas and Tamas which screen the light of Puruṣa are destroyed. Then the real nature of the Puruṣa is realized. Prāṇāyāma practice destroys the Karmas which hurl down man in various sorts of activities. Karmas also act as a screen that destroys the purity of intellect."

By the practice of prāṇāyāma, the mind becomes both quiet and alert, due to the decrease in rajas and tamas. It is only when the mind is sufficiently quiet and the gap between successive thoughts increasingly longer that we are able to become aware of our awareness (I AM). Our identity then shifts to being the silent witness (Sākṣī) that perceives or observes the movement of breath.

Prāṇāyāma, therefore, is a helpful precursor to concentration and meditation on the Self. In the following quote*, Śri Ramana Maharshi discusses the benefits of prāṇāyāma:

*"Prāṇayama is meant for one who cannot directly control the thoughts. It serves as a brake to a car. **But one should not stop with it but must proceed to pratyāhāra, dhāraṇā and dhyāna****. After the fruition of dhyāna, the mind will come under control even in the absence of Prāṇayama. The āsanas (postures) help Prāṇayama, which helps dhyāna in its turn, and peace of mind results. Here is the purpose of Haṭha Yoga."*

*Recorded in *Conscious Immortality* by Paul Brunton.
**Here, Śri Ramana Maharshi is referring to the next three limbs of yoga after this one (prāṇāyāma): pratyāhāra (withdrawal of the senses); dhāraṇā (concentration): and dhyāna (meditation).

In the next exercise, you will experience how the breath may be used very simply and safely for quieting the mind. It is based on yoga sūtra 1.34:

"Or, by maintaining the pensive state felt at the time of soft and steady exhalation and during passive retention after exhalation." [131]

In his commentary on this sūtra, B.K.S. Iyengar writes:

"One should inhale and exhale slowly and pause, maintaining the retention for as long as is comfortable. This practice ensures a state of consciousness which is like a calm lake."

This practice is a gentle one and can be fulfilled even if you have little or no experience of prāṇāyāma. It may be practiced when you are seated and just about to begin meditation. Swami Sivananda describes the benefits of practicing prāṇāyāma before meditation in the following quote:

"The mind acquires one-pointedness after the practice of Prāṇāyāma. Therefore you will have to take to Japa [repetition of a mantra] and meditation after Prāṇāyāma is over. Prāṇāyāma, though it is concerned with the breath, gives good exercise to the various internal organs, and the whole body. It is the best form of physical exercise every known." [132]

A cautionary note

There are many other prāṇāyāma techniques that originate from texts such as the Haṭha Yoga Pradīpikā. These should only be learnt under the guidance of a qualified teacher in order to prevent injury.

Self-enquiry and the Practice of Prāṇāyāma

Sit in your meditation posture with eyes closed. This method may also be carried out lying down. The suggested duration is ten minutes or longer.

Before starting, take a few full breaths, inhaling for the count of three and exhaling for the count of three. If possible, all inhalations and exhalations are to be through the nose.

Technique

1. After each complete exhalation, pause for one or two seconds. Never strain; take the next inhalation as soon

as you need to.

2.   When it feels right to do so, very gently allow the pause following each exhalation to gradually extend a little more. You will observe that as you do, the breath will become increasingly subtle and the mind, correspondingly quieter.

During the practice:
- Observe the rise and fall of the breath, allowing the mind to become very still.
- In the pause after each exhalation dive deep into your awareness. Identify with your awareness, the Ātman.

FIFTH LIMB

PRATYĀHĀRA
(Withdrawal of the Senses)

"The absorption of the mind in the Supreme Consciousness by realizing Ātman in all objects is known as Pratyāhāra (withdrawal of the mind) which should be practised by the seekers after liberation." ~ Aparokṣānubhūti (Verse 121)

PRATYĀHĀRA is defined in yoga sūtra 2.54 as:

"Withdrawing the senses, mind and consciousness from contact with external objects, and then drawing them inwards towards the Seer." [133]

The first aspect of pratyāhāra is related to when we sit for meditation. It often seems that no sooner do we close our eyes, we become bombarded with various thoughts and memories that appear as if from nowhere! This is a result of the many vāsānas stored in our subconscious mind. Pratyāhāra is the practice of actively bringing the mind back under control, toward the focal point of concentration.

During meditation, there needs to be both a firm conviction that you are the Witness (Self), and a simultaneous refusal to identify with the mind.

Over time, the practice of bringing the mind back again and again to the focal point of concentration develops the saṁskāras (habits) of restraint. The result is that the mind gradually gains mastery of itself, allowing the yogi to enter into samādhi or deep absorption in the Self. This process is the subject of yoga sūtras 3.9 to 3.11:

> *"Through the constant replacement of disturbing thought waves by ones of control, the mind is transformed and gains mastery of itself."*
>
> *"Its flow becomes undisturbed by repetition."*
>
> *"The transformation (leading to the ability to enter) samādhi comes gradually through the elimination of distractions and the rise of one-pointedness."* [134]

What about the time when we are not in seated meditation, the second aspect?

Pratyāhāra is the practice of cutting off the reaction of the imposter self to external objects, towards which we are to cultivate an attitude of detachment (vairagya).

When we identify with the Self within (Ātman or Brahman), this is how we will naturally begin to look upon everything else that appears to be external to us. What we perceive by our senses will start to feel more and more unreal to us — like a long dream from which we are meant to wake up.

As we become increasingly grounded in our identity as the Self, although we will still register objects by the senses, we become less and less distracted by them. We develop a quality of detachment toward all that which is impermanent.

In the following quote Ādi Śaṅkarācārya reminds us that the true nature of everything is Pure Consciousness:

> *"Oneself is what is within, oneself is without, oneself is in front and oneself is behind. Oneself is to the south, oneself is to the north, and oneself is also above and below."*
>
> ~ Vivekacūḍāmaṇi (Verse 389)

It is the ego or imposter self that tries to 'grasp' at objects of perception, reacting either positively or negatively, thus obscuring the Self.

To develop this level of pratyāhāra, the practice of seated meditation (seventh limb of yoga) is necessary for the vast majority of us. The importance of meditation was highlighted by Swami Chidananda when he said*:

"You have to do it by invoking the power of the Divine, and the one and only effective way of invoking the power of the Divine is through meditation. It is setting up a link — open a tap, and immediately there is a torrential flow of water. How? Because it is connected with a great storehouse of water; if that connection is not there, nothing is possible."

*In a talk recorded in Prerequisites for Knowledge, published by the Divine Life Society.

Similarly, Swami Vivekananda described meditation as: *"the greatest help to spiritual life"* and *"the bridge that connects the human soul to God"*.

The benefit of seated meditation is that the Self, one's Presence, becomes a current that is always there in the background, as we play our part in life.

Closed eye (seated) meditation, therefore, helps to facilitate this second aspect of Pratyāhāra — also a form of meditation, but with the eyes open — during daily life. For a while effort is required until it eventually becomes natural.

Ādi Śaṅkarācārya emphasized the need for constant meditation on the Self for final liberation. For example:

"The Ātman that is Absolute Existence and Knowledge cannot be realized without constant practice. So one seeking after knowledge should long meditate upon Brahman for the attainment of the desired goal". ~ Aparokṣānubhūti (Verse 101)

"This treasure of consciousness shines unfading with its own light as the witness of everything. Meditate continually

on it, making this your aim, distinct as it is from the unreal."
~ Vivekacūḍāmaṇi (Verse 380)
"This one should be aware of with unbroken application, continually turning to it with a mind empty of everything else, knowing it to be one's true nature." ~ Vivekacūḍāmaṇi (Verse 381)

Pause for Reflection

Reflect on how sensory inputs (taste, touch, smell, etc) are all objects of your awareness. Therefore, by turning your attention to that which is aware (the Witness) of sensory stimuli, there is a natural withdrawal away from external objects. Even thoughts are external objects in relation to the Self.

Lord Krishna tells us:

*"**'I do nothing at all'**, thus would the harmonized knower of truth think — seeing, hearing, touching, smelling, eating, going, sleeping, breathing."* ~ Bhagavad Gītā (Verse 5.8)

SIXTH LIMB

DHĀRAṆĀ (Concentration)

"The wise man who, by means of concentration on the Self, realizes that ancient, effulgent One, who is hard to be seen, unmanifest, hidden, and who dwells in the buddhi [intellect] and rests in the body – he, indeed, leaves joy and sorrow far behind." ~ Kaṭha Upaniṣad (Verse I.ii.12)

"I only beg you to test it, even at the cost of a little trouble. I assure you...you will find Him within you."
~ Saint Teresa of Avila

THE method of concentration given in this chapter is based on the following verse in Dṛg-Dṛśya-Viveka:

> *"Desire, etc* centered in the mind are to be treated as (cognizable) objects. Meditate on Consciousness as their Witness."* ~ Verse 24

> *"If one realizes that the thoughts arise from the Self and abide in their source, the mind will disappear."*
>
> ~ Śri Ramana Maharshi
> (Talks, 326)

*any thought, or mental modification arising in the mind

A couple of important points when practicing this method:

Do not try to fight with or destroy thoughts. It is natural for thoughts to arise, as Śri Ramana Maharshi explained while talking about the nature of the mind:

"It [mind] is accustomed to stray outward by the forces of the latent vāsanās manifesting as thoughts. So long as there are vāsanās contained within they must come out and exhaust themselves." ~ Talks, 326

At the same time do not engage with or attempt to continue any particular train of thought. The attitude towards any thought arising is to be one of indifference.

Also, try not to be discouraged if many thoughts arise! When Śri Ramana Maharshi (Talks, 28) was asked if it really is possible that all vāsanās can be destroyed, he responded:

"Yes. Many have done so. Believe it! They did so because they believed they could. Vāsanās (predispositions) can be obliterated. It is done by concentration on that which is free from vāsanās and yet is their core."

When asked how long it may take, he answered:

"Till success is achieved and until yoga-liberation becomes permanent. Success begets success. If one distraction is conquered the next is conquered and so on, until all are finally conquered. The process is like reducing an enemy's force by slaying its man-power — one by one, as each issues out."

Swami Sivananda also gives the following encouragement:

"Never become despondent at any stage of practice. You will surely get inner spiritual strength. You are bound to succeed in the end. All the Yogins of yore had to encounter the same difficulties that you are experiencing now. The process of destruction of mental modifications is difficult and long. All thoughts cannot be destroyed in a day or two. You should not give up the practice of destroying the thoughts in the middle when you come across some difficulties or stumbling blocks."[135]

Method: Self-enquiry and the Practice of Dhāraṇā

This method is to be carried out in a comfortable seated position, using a chair if needed. Closed eyes are necessary in order to turn the focus inwards. The recommended duration is a minimum of thirty minutes.

Read and familiarize yourself with the steps below and then begin:

1. When a thought arises in the mind, observe it, but with disinterest.
2. Now turn towards that which is aware of the thought — the background of awareness. As you do so, drop the thought.
3. Stay aware. Pay attention to your awareness only. Rest (abide) in the silence of the Self.

When another thought arises, repeat these steps.

Important Note

The idea is not to wait for thoughts to arise, but to use thought only as a means to reflect your attention back to the Self, and then abide as the Self. See also Part 1, Chapter 5 (Self-enquiry: Abiding in the Silence of the Self).

After some days, weeks, or months of practicing this method of concentration, you will be able to close your eyes and immediately rest in your own awareness (Self). This is not to say that thoughts no longer arise. But it does mean that your practice of concentration has now developed into meditation on the Self. There should now be a sense of effortlessness in the practice.

SEVENTH LIMB

DHYĀNA (Meditation)

*"Yoga is in its strictest sense Meditation
on the Absolute Reality."* ~ Swami Krishnananda [136]

*"Seek and you will find; knock and the door
will be opened to you."* ~ Matthew 7:7

WE HAVE now arrived at the most important limb of yoga, concerning meditation.

Swami Tejomayananda, a direct disciple of Swami Chinmayananda, defines meditation as the "Effortless Awareness" of one's true nature:*

"To define Meditation — 'Of one's true nature, an **effortless awareness'** — that is what it is. It is not a particular action, nor is it worship of the Lord with attributes, or chanting** of His Name."*

> *"Meditation on the immortal Self will act like a dynamite and blow up all thoughts and memories in the conscious mind. If the thoughts trouble you much, do not try to suppress them by force. Be a silent witness as in a bioscope. They will subside gradually. Then route them out through regular silent meditation."*
>
> ~ Swami Sivananda [137]

*From Dhyana-Swaroopam – The Nature of Meditation (Verse 1).

**If you currently have a meditation practice using a mantra, I am not advocating that you give up this practice.

A suggestion is that this be continued as a separate concentration practice.

The sole purpose of putting into practice all that we have covered is that Self-enquiry, in addition to the previous six limbs of yoga, enables you to rest effortlessly in your own awareness (I AM) — even though thoughts may still arise. A good meditation, however, is one in which there are no thoughts. Effortless awareness of one's true nature is the fourth type of focus (asmitā*) listed in yoga sūtra 1.17.

*Ādi Śaṅkarācārya, in his commentary on the yoga sūtras, points out that asmitā here is not the same as the asmitā listed as one of the obstacles (kleśas) to yoga in yoga sūtra 2.3. The latter is equivalent to the I-thought or ego (ahaṁkāra). Asmitā in sūtra 1.17, however, refers to the I AM (the Witness). See also Part 1, Chapter 10.

I am now referring to seated meditation, in which there is a steadiness or firmness of the body. That the posture is to be a seated one is specified not only by Patañjali, but also Śri Vyāsa, author of The Brahma Sūtras (see Chapter IV-Section 1 Sūtras 7-10).

Seated meditation (with the eyes closed) is necessary as it allows the mind to sufficiently subside so that one's attention is able to turn inwards.

> *"This is the supreme meditation, this is the supreme worship: the continuous and unbroken awareness of the indwelling presence, inner light or consciousness."*
>
> ~ Yoga-Vāsiṣṭha[138]

Meditation is to be continued right up to the point of Self-realization (final liberation), as emphasized in The Brahma Sūtras (plus associated commentary). For example:

*"Meditation should be continued till the last trace of body idea is destroyed. When the **body consciousness is totally***

annihilated, *Brahman shines itself in all its pristine glory and purity. The meditator and the meditated become one. Individuality vanishes in toto."* [139]

The process by which the Self is realized begins with listening to the teachings and being guided in the process of Self-enquiry to uncover your true nature. But this has to be both deeply reflected upon and then assimilated in meditation. The latter leads to absorption in Brahman (samādhi). This process is summarized in the following quote by Swami Nikhilananda:

"In order that the Knowledge of Brahman may be realized directly and clearly, 'like a fruit on the palm of one's hand', and not merely understood intellectually, Vedānta prescribes certain disciplines, known as 'hearing' (śravaṇam), 'reflecting' (mananam), 'meditating' (nididhyāsanam), and 'absorption in Brahman' (samādhi). 'Hearing' means listening to the instruction of a qualified teacher, who explains from the scriptures the oneness of the Individual self and Brahman. 'Reflecting' means thinking constantly of Brahman thus taught, and strengthening one's conviction regarding Its reality by means of suitable reasoning."

"Meditation, practised uninterruptedly for a long time with intense love for the ideal and with unflagging determination for its realization leads to samādhi, or absorption in Brahman." [140]

Meditation on the Self is the greatest of all meditations. Lord Krishna instructs:

"Little by little let him attain to quietude by the intellect held firmly; having made the mind establish itself in the Self, let him not think of anything." ~ Verse 6.25

In his commentary on this verse, Ādi Śaṅkarācārya writes:

*"He should make the mind constantly abide in the Self, bearing in mind that the Self is all and that nothing else exists. **This is the highest form of Yoga.**"*

Śri Ramana Maharshi also said of this form of meditation:

"Since the Self is the reality of all gods, the meditation on the Self which is oneself is the greatest of all meditations. All other meditations are included in this. It is for gaining this that the other meditations are prescribed. So if this is gained, the others are not necessary. Knowing that there is a deity which is different and meditating on it, is compared by the great ones to the act of measuring with one's foot one's own shadow, and to the search for a trivial conch after throwing away a priceless gem that is already in one's possession." [141]

Similarly, Swami Vidyāraṇya, the author of Pañcadaśī, writes:

"As by meditation on the Personal God knowledge of the nature of Īśvara arises, so by meditation on the attributeless Brahman, knowledge of Its nature arises and destroys the ignorance which is the root of rebirth." ~ Verse IX.140

The meditation technique given in this section is, in essence, the same as the method for abiding in the Self in Part 1 Chapter 5. We must now, however, give full importance to the following instruction given in The Brahma Sūtras:

> *"Brahman is not grasped by the eye, nor by speech, nor by the other senses, nor by penance or good works. A man becomes pure through serenity of intellect; thereupon, in meditation, he beholds Him who is without parts."*
>
> ~ Muṇḍaka Upaniṣad (Verse III.i.8)

"He who meditates on the Supreme Brahman must comprehend it as identical with himself." [142]

In the associated commentary it is explained:

"The individual is essentially Brahman only. The Jivahood is due to the limiting adjunct, the internal organ or Antaḥ-karaṇa [mind/intellect]. The Jivahood is illusory. The Jiva is in reality an embodiment of bliss. It experiences pain and misery on account of the limiting adjunct, Antaḥkaraṇa.... Hence we must fix our minds on Brahman as being the Self." [143]

> **"Without the help of meditation, you cannot attain knowledge of the Self. Without its aid, you cannot grow into the divine state. Without it, you cannot liberate your self from the trammels of the mind and attain immortality."**
>
> ~ Swami Sivananda [144]

There are two further 'secret' ingredients to this meditation that we will now consider. The first relates to the focal point for our meditation. The scriptures speak of Brahman or the Self residing in the 'cave of the heart'. Swami Nikhilananda discusses this in the following quote:

"In the subjective meditation the Ideal is placed within oneself. Vedāntic seers speak of the heart as an extremely suitable place. For the beginner the heart is the physical organ, shaped like a lotus-bud. Inside there is a subtle, luminous space which is often described as Brahmapura, the abode of Brahman. As he makes progress in meditation and becomes capable of subtle perceptions, he realizes that the heart denotes not really the physical organ but the, buddhi, the determinative faculty, which is the most refined part of the mind and in which one sees best the reflection of Brahman." [145]

The 'heart' then refers to the very core of one's being — the seat of love and the other noble qualities of compassion, etc.

The second, even more important ingredient is bhakti, one's

love for the highest ideal. We can nurture this love by bringing to mind one who embodies this ideal, such as one's guru (for example, Śrī Ramana Maharshi, etc) or chosen deity (Lord Krishna, Lord Śiva, Jesus, Buddha, etc).

This bhakti must be combined with the utter faith (śraddhā) or firm conviction in both the means to the goal and the goal itself. Together, śraddhā and bhakti give single pointedness in meditation (dhyāna) and eventual union (yoga) with the Supreme.

When the sage Āshvalāyana approached Lord Brahma* to ask how he is to attain the highest knowledge, the Lord replied:

"Attain it through faith (śraddhā), devotion (bhakti), meditation (dhyāna) and yoga." ~ Kaivalya Upaniṣad (Verse 2)

*The Creator in the Hindu Trinity. Not to be confused with Brahman.

One final clarification:

Many devotes would ask Śrī Ramana Maharshi questions on the subject of meditation, and whether meditation on the attributeless Brahman is the same as repeating mentally the Mahāvākya (great sentence) 'I am Brahman' ('aham brahmāsmi'). One of his replies was:

> *"In a heart in which true love is overflowing, it will be known clearly that one's own nature is nothing but bliss."*
>
> ~ Padamalai (Verse 128)

"'I am Brahman' is only a thought. Who says it? Brahman himself does not say so. What need is there for Him to say it? Nor can the real 'I' say so, for 'I' always abides as Brahman. To be saying it is only a thought. Whose thought is it? All thoughts are from the unreal 'I', i.e., the 'I'-thought. Remain without thinking." ~ Talks, 202

Meditation on the Self (the attributeless Brahman)

It is suggested that you begin with a minimum of 30 to 60

minutes of daily meditation – if possible, both morning and evening. This is to be gradually increased.

Preliminaries:

- First find a comfortable seated position in a place where you will not be disturbed.
- The spine should be erect - the back, neck and head in one line.
- Close the eyes.
- Begin by releasing all tension in the face and body. Pay particular attention to the shoulders, releasing all tension from this area.
- Breathe normally. Remain as still as you can, without being rigid.

Practice:

- Invoke the presence of your guru (or chosen deity) in your heart center with love and reverence (see hints in Note 1 below).
- Turn your attention (180 degrees inward) away from the world, body, and mind towards the Self.
- Give attention to the Self alone, with single minded devotion.
- Ignore all thought. If thought arises, turn your attention to that which is aware (the Witness) of thought.

Notes:

1. For example, you may wish to mentally bow down to your guru/the Lord and ask for His/Her blessings. You may also, after surrendering all your attachments (your wants and needs, difficulties, etc) at the feet of the guru/the Lord, visualize Him/Her taking your hand to enter the sacred cave of the heart at the very core of your being.

2. The initial tendency of the mind is to try and 'grasp' one's awareness as if it were an object. Hence the need for both mental relaxation and alertness.

3. This meditation should feel like a letting-go or turning-away from everything that is not the Self. This includes all perceivable objects, both subtle (thoughts, memories, emotions, experiences, etc) and gross (external physical objects which includes the body).

4. It is not helpful to question one's own progress or anticipate certain results or mystical experiences. Only Īśvara has knowledge of the vāsanās remaining and all our (the jivas) exit points from the dream of separation. Our job is to abide in the Self and surrender the outcome to God. The meditation practice itself is the progress.

With commitment and consistency in your practice of meditation, eventual success is guaranteed. This is the subject of the following verse from Swami Vidyāraṇya's Pañcadaśī.

"(The Self as if says): 'Even if direct knowledge of Me does not seem to be possible, a man should still meditate on the Self. In the course of time, he doubtlessly realizes the Self and is freed.'" ~ Verse IX.152

It is, therefore, impossible to fail. Although the Ātman is actionless, the effect of its very Presence as we turn toward it may be compared to the effect that a magnet has on iron filings. We cannot help but be drawn inward.

In the following verse, Lord Krishna promises that only willingness and effort on our part is required, He will do the rest.

"Fix thy mind on Me, be devoted to Me, sacrifice to Me, bow down to Me. Thou shalt come to Me; truly do I promise unto thee, (for) thou art dear to Me." ~ Bhagavad Gītā (Verse 18.65)

Coming out of Meditation

When not practising seated closed-eye meditation, our practice is to continuously feel our oneness with the all-pervading Brahman, denying the body and world as an appearance only. Swami Sivananda explains:

> *"Another important point is that the Brahmic feeling must be kept up all twenty-four hours. There must be an unceasing continuous flow of consciousness. You must not forget the idea of 'Aham Brahma Āsmi' or the Divine presence even for a single second. Forgetfulness of God is genuine death. It is real suicide."* [146]

The mental repetition of Om, or another personal mantra, is an aid for this.

Some further advice is also given by Swami Chidananda in his talk The Essence of Sādhana*, in which he spoke of the practice of concluding the daily morning meditation, in the presence of Swami Sivananda, with a chant, the meaning of which is:

> *"Salutations to the Infinite, the One with a thousand forms, with a thousand feet, thousand eyes, thousand heads, thousand thighs and thousand arms. Salutations to the One who has a thousand names, who is the Eternal Person, who supports the thousands of crores of ages."*

*Talk given at Śri Samadhi Mandir on 20/9/91, recorded in pamphlet: Sādhana — the Keynote of Gurudev's Teachings.

Of this customary practice Swami Chidananda explained in his talk:

> *"Thus when the meditator, who has been meditating upon the one great Reality, the supreme, imponderable eternal Truth, the ultimate Divine Being who alone exists, when he comes out of the contemplation of this Ekam eva advitīyam Brahma (Brahman, the One without a second), the Antarātmā (inner*

Self), what does he do? He makes the necessary provision so that this inner contemplation of the supreme Divine Reality is not lost. This deep meditation, the inner dwelling on the Divine, is meant to smoothly continue in the waking state also, even when one is aware of all the multifarious names and forms in the outer environment."

"This means that I behold all forms as His forms. Everywhere He is. He alone has taken this Cosmic Form."

"Thus inner meditation is smoothly made to prevail in the waking state. It is to continue. Nothing is to change. God is beheld in and through the world. The vision of the world is then succeeded by: You are my mother, You are my father. You are my relative and friend. You are my knowledge and my wealth. You are my all in all."

This is also beautifully expressed in the Br̥hadāraṇyaka Upaniṣad, where it is said:

"It is not for the love of a husband that a husband is dear; but for the love of the Self in the husband that a husband is dear.

It is not for the love of a wife that a wife is dear; but for the love of the Self in the wife that a wife is dear.

It is not for the love of children that children are dear; but for the love of the Self in children that children are dear.

It is not for the love of all that all is dear; but for the love of the Self in all that all is dear." ~ Verse II.iv.4

Obstacles to Meditation

This chapter would not be complete without a brief mention of the main obstacles to meditation, along with some practical suggestions on how to manage them. The obstacles are:

i.   Stupor/sleepiness (laya)

This is a common obstacle, and a very frustrating one, especially when we first start out in meditation. It is due to force of habit — the mind is trained to associate closing the eyes with sleep. A way to overcome this obstacle is to introduce thought, for example, by contemplating one of the Mahāvākyas or sentences from the Upaniṣads (see example given on page 165). This helps the mind become alert again.

ii. Mental distractions/agitations (Vikṣepa)

Various thoughts may arise during meditation. This is another very common obstacle. Each time you notice that the mind has become engaged in thought, bring it back to the focal point of concentration. This is the practice of pratyāhāra (fifth limb) discussed earlier which goes hand in hand with the art of concentration.

At times during meditation, you may find that your mind becomes agitated about external matters. For example, perhaps the desire arises to check your phone for e-mails, etc. The solution here is self-effort to counteract and not give-in to these tendencies. Tell the mind that mental agitations arise only due to our past habits and tendencies which no longer serve us. Take what discerning measures you can to prevent such distractions, for example: turn your phone off; do not look at the news before you meditate; have a 'do not disturb' sign on your door, etc.

Above all, do not be discouraged! It is not uncommon for meditation to feel rather like 'bitter medicine', especially when we try to increase the duration. Careful self-effort is required here – increase the time gradually, perhaps only five or ten minutes at a time to stop the mind from rebelling.

iii. 'Blocking Dirt' (Kashāya)

In Part 1 Chapter 10, I described how a mind purified of rajas and tamas may be compared to a transparent crystal or clean mirror. The result is that the Self-effulgent consciousness 'reveals' itself, thereby 'filling' the mind. It reveals itself not as an object of experience but as your very Being.

The 'blocking dirt' of subtle, deep rooted saṁskāras/vāsanās is an obstacle to this and prevents the attainment of the lower (samprajñātā) samādhi (described further in the next limb). During meditation, this obstacle may manifest in the following manner: your mind is quiet (no thoughts), but more as an inert blankness or void-like state.

The solution here is to be patient. You are on the right track — have no doubt about it! Keep your attention on the consciousness that is aware of the blankness or void. Be rest assured that it is the meditation itself that scrubs away the 'dirt' on the mirror mind. Sooner or later, you will get glimpses of your true nature.

iv. Taste of Bliss (Rasāsvāda)

This is the most subtle obstacle as it is the obstacle to asamprajñātā or nirvikalpa samādhi. Rasāsvāda refers to attachment to the bliss of samprajñātā samādhi and is to be counteracted by viveka (discrimination). Do not be satisfied with the experience of bliss — it is only a reflection of the bliss of Reality.

You are getting close to your goal! Now is the time to increase your efforts in meditation even more, devoting as much time as your daily responsibilities allow you to.

EIGHTH LIMB

SAMĀDHI (Absorption in Brahman)

"Reflection [mananam] should be considered a hundred times superior to hearing [śravaṇam], and meditation [ṇididhyāsanam] a hundred thousand times superior even to reflection, but the Nirvikalpa Samādhi is infinite in its results." ~ Vivekacūḍāmaṇi (Verse 364)

"If thine eye be single, thy whole body will be filled with light." ~ Matthew 6.22

BY uninterrupted meditation on the Self, the mind eventually takes the form of I AM (asmitā) alone. Such a state of one-pointed absorption is saṁprajñātā samādhi (also known as savikalpa samādhi).

> *"Brahman can be clearly and definitely realized only through Nirvikalpa Samādhi. Samādhi ensues only when the purified mind is merged in Brahman."*
>
> ~ Swami Sivananda[147]

It is from saṁprajñātā samādhi, that the yogi, through identification with Para Brahman - the Pure/Original Consciousness from whom the mind borrows its light, goes on to attain asaṁprajñātā samādhi (also known as nirvikalpa samādhi).

The attainment of asaṁprajñātā samādhi, however, is not through human effort but only what can best be described as ultimate renunciation.

The objectless state of asamprajñātā samādhi — in which the world does not exist for the meditator — is described in yoga sūtra 1.3:

"Then the Seer dwells in his own true splendour." [148]

The difference between samprajñātā and asamprajñātā samādhi is that in samprajñātā samādhi, the yogi is aware of the pure reflection of Brahman (Original/Pure Consciousness). In asamprajñātā samādhi, there is cessation of even this last cognitive act.

With asamprajñātā (nirvikalpa) samādhi comes the complete annihilation of the last remaining vāsanās. Swami Sivananda explains:

"There is no Vāsanā in Brahman. Complete annihilation of the Vāsanās takes place only in Nirvikalpa Samādhi. Only Nirvikalpa Samādhi can completely fry up the seeds of impure Vāsanās. Through the knowledge of Brahman, there will be an extinction of all Vāsanās, which form the medium of enjoyments. With the extinction of all Vāsanās, the undaunted mind will get quiescence like a gheeless lamp." [149]

> **"The forces of intense meditation lights up the entire materialized nature and at once liberates the soul like a sudden flash of lightening. At one stroke the universe dwindles into nothingness and the Majesty of Brahman is revealed. This is the Goal."**
>
> ~ Swami Krishnananda [150]

In the following quote, Swami Krishnananda describes the annihilation of the mind (manonāśa) that occurs in asamprajñātā (nirvikalpa) samādhi:

"When the Self is asserted to be in tune with the Great Expanse of the Reality the mind which is a shadow of the Self turns back to its substance, the Self.

The mind vanishes for want of objects of perception. When

the One Brahman alone is seen everywhere, where is the occasion for the appearance of objects?" [151]

As a result, ignorance (avidyā) and its effects, Kama (desire) and Karma (action) are destroyed for all of eternity. This is Self-realization or kaivalya.

For final liberation (Self-realization) the mind must be completely extinguished — there cannot be any chance of its resurrection. Swami Krishnananda explains:

"The Sankalpas [thoughts] should be destroyed beyond resurrection. The resuscitation of Vāsanās allows the tree of Saṃsāra to grow once again and therefore, the purpose of all methods of Yoga is the utter removal of all the possibilities of further appearances of the mind." [152]

Swami Nikhilananda further explains:

"Vedāntic seers say that one cannot attain complete Freedom and Knowledge in life by experiencing the nirvikalpa samādhi once or twice. Only by repeated practice can one become established in Brahman and rid oneself of all the vestiges of māyā. The seed of ignorance must be fully roasted in the fire of Brahmajñāna [direct knowledge of Brahman]." [153]

The state of kaivalya or Self-realization is described in the very last yoga sūtra (4.34).

"Kaivalya is that state in which the guṇas (attain equilibrium and) merge in their cause, having no longer a purpose in relation to Puruṣa. The Soul is established in its True Nature, which is Pure Consciousness. End." [154]

Concluding Note

Ultimately success in yoga comes down to how intensely we desire liberation. Yoga sūtra 1.21, tells us:

"The goal is near for those who are supremely vigorous and intense in practice." [155]

This is also the subject of the followng verse from Padamalai*:

"The glory of self-realization is not experienced except in the hearts of those who are very zealous about sinking into the Self." ~ Verse 80

*By Sri Murugunar, a devotee of Śri Ramana Maharshi.

For this, more intense and prolonged meditation is required. And then? Swami Chidananda describes the indescribable*:

"You become liberated from all the pains of Saṃsāra [cycle of birth and death], as it were, and become established or enter into a state of indescribable felicity, happiness, supreme joy, and become liberated from the necessity of once again coming into this embodied state; no more birth into this phenomenal world. In that state of freedom, liberated from birth and death, sorrow, pain and suffering, you enter into a state of absolute bliss. Your entire being is filled with supreme, eternal satisfaction. That is the use, that is the result of attaining God-experience or Self-realisation. It fills you with supreme bliss."

*From a lecture recorded in the e-book *Bliss is Within*.

INDEX OF REFERENCES

Introduction

1. Maharshi's Gospel; Sri Ramanasramam Tiruvannamalai 13th ed (2002); Book 1, Chapter 2; p. 15.
2. B.K.S. Iyengar. Light on the Yoga Sūtras of Patañjali; Thorsons (2002); p. 113.
3. Swami Venkatesananda. Vāsiṣṭha's Yoga; State University of New York Press (1993); p. 322.
4. B.K.S. Iyengar. Light on Life The Journey to Wholeness, Inner Peace and Ultimate Freedom; Rodale 1st ed (2005); p. 8.
5. B.K.S. Iyengar. Light on the Yoga Sūtras of Patañjali; Thorsons (2002); p. 101.
6. B.K.S. Iyengar. Light on the Yoga Sūtras of Patañjali; Thorsons (2002); p. 135.

PART 1 – SELF-ENQUIRY

Chapter 1: The Seer and the Seen

7. Michael Langford. Powerful Quotes from Sankara; The Freedom Religion Press (2012); p. 60.
8. Talks with Sri Ramana Maharshi; Sri Ramanasramam Tiruvannamalai (2006); Talks, 454.
9. Swami Vishnu-Devananda. Meditation and Mantras, Motilal Banarsidass Publishers 6th ed (2013); p. 203.
10. Sivananda Upanishad A Universal Scripture in the Sage's Own Handwriting; Om Lotus Publishing Inc. (2007); p. 430.

Chapter 2: Enquiry into the Five Sheaths

11. Thomas Byrom. The Heart of Awareness A Translation of the Ashtavakra; Shambhala Dragon Editions (2001); p. 4.
12. Swami Sivananda. Vedanta for Beginners; The Divine Life Society 6th ed (2016); p. 48.

Chapter 3: Enquiry into the Ego

13. Talks with Sri Ramana Maharshi; Sri Ramanasramam Tiruvannamalai (2006); Talks, 427.

14. B.K.S. Iyengar. Light on the Yoga Sūtras of Patañjali; Thorsons (2002); p. 250.

15. Michael Langford. How Not to Get Lost in Concepts; The Freedom Religion Press (2011); Page 35.

16. Talks with Sri Ramana Maharshi; Sri Ramanasramam Tiruvannamalai (2006); Talks, 347.

17. David Godman. Be As You are: The Teachings of Sri Ramana Maharshi; Arkana (1985); p. 49.

Chapter 4: Self-Enquiry by Subject-Object Discrimination

18. Michael Langford. Powerful Quotes from Sankara; The Freedom Religion Press (2012); p. 64.

19. Thomas Byrom. The Heart of Awareness A Translation of the Ashtavakra; Shambhala Dragon Editions (2001); p. 1.

20. Swami Tejomayananda. Tattva Vivekah Chapter -1 Pañcadaśī; Central Chinmaya Mission Trust (2012); p. 22.

Chapter 5: Self-Enquiry – Abiding in the Silence of the Self

21. Michael Langford. The Seven Steps to Awakening; The Freedom Religion Press (2015); p. 11.

22. Michael Langford. The Seven Steps to Awakening; The Freedom Religion Press (2015); p. 189.

23. Michael Langford. The Seven Steps to Awakening; The Freedom Religion Press (2015); p. 187.

Chapter 6: Discrimination Between the Permanent and the Transient

24. Michael Langford. Everything is an Illusion; The Freedom Religion Press (2011); p. 82.

25. Michael Langford. Everything is an Illusion; The Freedom Religion Press (2011); p. 9.

26. Thomas Byrom. The Heart of Awareness A Translation of the Ashtavakra; Shambhala Dragon Editions (2001); p. 5.

27. B.K.S. Iyengar. Light on the Yoga Sūtras of Patañjali; Thorsons (2002); p. 113-4.

28. B.K.S. Iyengar. Light on the Yoga Sūtras of Patañjali; Thorsons (2002); p. 136-7.

29. Swami Venkatesananda. Vāsiṣṭha's Yoga; State University of New York Press (1993); p. 5.

Chapter 7: Negation of the False ('Neti' Neti')

30. Michael Langford. Powerful Quotes from Sankara; The Freedom Religion Press (2012); p. 61.

31. Swami Nikhilananda. Self-Knowledge of Sri Sankaracarya; Sri Ramakrishna Math (2015); p. 124.

Chapter 8: How the Impossible Appeared to Happen

32. Swami Venkatesananda. Vāsiṣṭha's Yoga; State University of New York Press (1993); p. 48.

33. Swami Venkatesananda. Vāsiṣṭha's Yoga; State University of New York Press (1993); p. 52.

34. Swami Sivananda. Self-Knowledge; Divine Life Society World Wide Web (WWW) Edition (2002); p. 1.

35. Swami Sivananda. Brahma Sūtras; The Divine Life Society 4th ed (2008); Commentary to verse I.1.5; p.23.

36. Swami Nikhilananda. The Upanishads Volume I; Harper & Brothers Publishers, New York (1949); Commentary to Kaṭha Upaniṣad Verses I.iii.10-11; p. 152.

37. Swami Sivananda. Vedanta for Beginners; The Divine Life Society 6th ed (2016); p. 19.

38. Swami Nikhilananda. The Upanishads Volume I; Harper & Brothers Publishers, New York (1949); Discussion of Brahman; p. 58.

39. Swami Sivananda. The Moksha Gita Commentary by Swami Krishnananda; The Divine Life Society eBook edition; p. 41.

40. Swami Nikhilananda. Self-Knowledge of Sri Sankaracarya; Sri Ramakrishna Math (2015); p. 60.

41. Swami Nikhilananda. The Upanishads Volume I; Harper & Brothers Publishers, New York (1949); Discussion on Brahman; p. 74.

42. Swami Sivananda. Brahma Sūtras; The Divine Life Society 4th ed (2008); Commentary to verse II.3.13; p. 251.

43. Swami Sivananda. Brahma Sūtras; The Divine Life Society 4th ed (2008); Topic 6 (Sutras 14 to 20); p. 160.

44. Swami Sivananda. Brahma Sūtras; The Divine Life Society 4th ed (2008); Introduction; p. 5.

45. Swami Sivananda. Vedanta for Beginners; The Divine Life Society 6th ed (2016); p. 30-31.

46. Thomas Byrom. The Heart of Awareness A Translation of the Ashtavakra; Shambhala Dragon Editions (2001); p. 20.

47. Swami Nikhilananda. The Upanishads Volume II; Harper & Brothers Publishers, New York (1952); Gauḍapāda Kārikā verse III.29; p. 300.

48. Swami Sivananda. Vedanta for Beginners; The Divine Life Society 6th ed (2016); p. 23.

49. The Complete Works of Swami Vivekananda, Volume 2, Jnana Yoga.

Chapter 9: All this is Brahman

50. Thomas Byrom. The Heart of Awareness A Translation of the Ashtavakra; Shambhala Dragon Editions (2001); p. 5.

51. *https://www.sivanandaonline.org/public_html/?cmd=displaysection§ion_id=814&parent=684&format=html*

52. Thomas Byrom. The Heart of Awareness A Translation of the Ashtavakra; Shambhala Dragon Editions (2001); p. 17.

53. The Bhagavad Gītā Text, Word-to-Word Meaning Translation and Commentary by Swami Sivananda; The Divine Life Society 11th ed (2003); Chapter 18, commentary to Verse 66; p. 516.

54. Swami Sivananda. Brahma Sūtras; The Divine Life Society 4th ed (2008); commentary to verse I.3.1; p. 79.

Chapter 10: Who Am I?

55. A. Devarja Mudaliar. Day By Day With Bhagavan; Sri Ramanasramam Tiruvannamalai 1st ed (2011); Day 18-7-46.

56. Swami Sivananda. Vedanta for Beginners; The Divine Life Society 6th ed (2016); p. 121.

57. Swami Nikhilananda. Dṛg-Dṛśya-Viveka An Inquiry into the Nature of the 'Seer' and the 'Seen'; Sri Ramakrishna Asrama Mysore (1931); commentary to verse 9; p. 12.

58. Michael Langford. Powerful Quotes from Sankara; The Freedom Religion Press (2012); p. 53.

59. Edwin F. Bryant. The Yoga Sūtras of Patañjali; North Point Press (2009); p. 403.

60. Michael Langford. The Seven Steps to Awakening; The Freedom Religion Press (2015); p. 190.

61. Michael Langford. How to Practice Self-inquiry; The Freedom Religion Press (2014); p. 50.

62. B.K.S. Iyengar. Light on the Yoga Sūtras of Patañjali; Thorsons (2002); p. 86.

Chapter 11: Īśvara - God in the Dream of Separation

63. Who Am I? The Teachings of Bhagavan Sri Ramana Maharshi; Sri Ramanasramam Tiruvannamalai (2010); p. 28.

64. The Bhagavad Gītā Text, Word-to-Word Meaning Translation and Commentary by Swami Sivananda; The Divine Life Society 11th ed (2003); Chapter 7, commentary to Verse 6; p. 160.

65. Swami Sivananda. Vedanta for Beginners; The Divine Life Society 6th ed (2016); p. 89.

66. B.K.S. Iyengar. Light on the Yoga Sūtras of Patañjali; Thorsons (2002); p. 130-131.

67. B.K.S. Iyengar. Light on the Yoga Sūtras of Patañjali; Thorsons (2002); p. 130.
68. B.K.S. Iyengar. Light on the Yoga Sūtras of Patañjali; Thorsons (2002); p. 125.
69. Swami Sivananda. *https://www.dlshq.org/religions/darsanas.htm*
70. Swami Sivananda. Raja Yoga; The Divine Life Society 7th ed (2016); p. 19.
71. Swami Sivananda. *https://www.dlshq.org/religions/darsanas.htm*
72. Swami Sivananda. *https://www.dlshq.org/saints/sankara.htm*

Chapter 12: The Uncomfortable Truth

73. Thomas Byrom. The Heart of Awareness A Translation of the Ashtavakra; Shambhala Dragon Editions (2001); p. 13.
74. Michael Langford. The Seven Steps to Awakening; The Freedom Religion Press (2015); p. 85.
75. Michael Langford. The Seven Steps to Awakening; The Freedom Religion Press (2015); p. 85.
76. Jan Frazier. The Freedom of Being: At Ease with What Is; Weiser Books (2012); p. 63.

Chapter 13: Manonāśa — When the Mind Becomes No-mind

77. Swami Sivananda. Thought Power; The Divine Life Society 15th ed (2007); p. 6.
78. Swami Sivananda. *http://sivanandaonline.org/public_html/?cmd=displ aysection§ion_id=884*
79. B.K.S. Iyengar. Light on the Yoga Sūtras of Patañjali; Thorsons (2002); p. 121.
80. Swami Sivananda. Thought Power; The Divine Life Society 15th ed (2007); p. 78.
81. Swami Sivananda. Thought Power; The Divine Life Society 15th ed (2007); p. 14-15.
82. B.K.S. Iyengar. Light on the Yoga Sūtras of Patañjali; Thorsons (2002); p. 123.
83. Michael Langford. The Seven Steps to Awakening; The Freedom Religion Press (2015); p. 190.
84. Maharshi's Gospel; Sri Ramanasramam Tiruvannamalai 13th ed (2002); Book 2, Chapter 3; p. 61.
85. Swami Nikhilananda. The Upanishads Volume II; Harper & Brothers Publishers, New York (1952); Adaptation of Śankara's commentary on GAU.KĀ. I. 17; p. 242.
86. Swami Sivananda. The Moksha Gita; The Divine Life Society e-book; p. 60.

87. Who Am I? The Teachings of Bhagavan Sri Ramana Maharshi; Sri Ramanasramam Tiruvannamalai (2010); p. 16.

88. Annamalai Swami: Final Talks Edited by David Godman; Annamalai Swami Ashram; p.51.

89. Sri Guru Ramana Prasadam by Muruganar; Robert Butler; verse 555.

PART 2 - YOGA

Introduction

90. Thomas Byrom. The Heart of Awareness A Translation of the Ashtavakra; Shambhala Dragon Editions (2001); p. 65.

91. B.K.S. Iyengar. Light on the Yoga Sūtras of Patañjali; Thorsons (2002); p. 139-140.

92. *https://chinmaya-boston.org/pgswami-chinmayananda-articles/kill-the-ego/*

93. Thomas Byrom. The Heart of Awareness A Translation of the Ashtavakra; Shambhala Dragon Editions (2001); p. 10.

94. B.K.S. Iyengar. Light on the Yoga Sūtras of Patañjali; Thorsons (2002); p. 108.

95. B.K.S. Iyengar. Light on the Yoga Sūtras of Patañjali; Thorsons (2002); p. 66.

96. *http://sivanandaonline.org/public_html/?cmd=displaysection§ion_id=1518*

First Limb: Yamas (Moral Restraints)

97. Towards Perfection (*sivanandaonline.org*)

98. Thus Spake the Holy Mother; Sri Ramakrishna Math; p. 72-73.

99. Swami Saradeshananda. "The Holy Mother's Reminiscences". Vedanta Kesari.

100. Michael Langford. Powerful Quotes from Sankara; The Freedom Religion Press (2012); p. 41.

101. Swami Sivananda. Thought Power; The Divine Life Society 15th ed (2007); p. 24-25.

102. Swami Tapasyananda, Swami Nikhilananda. Sri Sarada Devi, the Holy Mother; Life and Conversations; Sri Ramakrishna Math; p. 292.

Second Limb: Niyamas (Self-disciplines)

103. Self-Enquiry of Bhagavan Sri Ramana Maharshi; Sri Ramanasramam Tiruvannamalai (1990).

104. Michael Langford. Powerful Quotes from Sankara; The Freedom Religion Press (2012); p. 8.

105. The Bhagavad Gītā Text, Word-to-Word Meaning Translation and Commentary by Swami Sivananda; The Divine Life Society 11th ed (2003); Chapter 13, commentary to Verse 7; p. 325.

106. Swami Sivananda. Thought Power; The Divine Life Society 15th ed (2007); p. 99.

107. B.K.S. Iyengar. Light on the Yoga Sūtras of Patañjali; Thorsons (2002); p. 154.

108. The Bhagavad Gītā Text, Word-to-Word Meaning Translation and Commentary by Swami Sivananda; The Divine Life Society 11th ed (2003); Chapter 16, commentary to Verse 1; p. 411.

109. Swami Venkatesananda. Vāsiṣṭha's Yoga; State University of New York Press (1993); p. 133.

110. Michael Langford. Powerful Quotes from Sankara; The Freedom Religion Press (2012); p. 45.

111. Swami Venkatesananda. Vāsiṣṭha's Yoga; State University of New York Press (1993); p. 273.

112. Swami Sivananda. Bliss Divine; The Divine Life Society 10th ed (2017); p. 147.

113. Swami Sivananda. Bliss Divine; The Divine Life Society 10th ed (2017); p. 146.

114. Swami Nikhilananda. The Upanishads Volume II; Harper & Brothers Publishers, New York (1952); commentary on Māṇḍūkya Upaniṣad (verse 1); p. 223.

115. Self-Enquiry of Bhagavan Sri Ramana Maharshi; Sri Ramanasramam Tiruvannamalai (1990).

116. Swami Tapasyananda, Swami Nikhilananda. Śri Sarada Devi, the Holy Mother; Life and Conversations; Sri Ramakrishna Math; p. 348.

117. Self-Enquiry of Bhagavan Sri Ramana Maharshi; Sri Ramanasramam Tiruvannamalai (1990).

118. B.K.S. Iyengar. Light on the Yoga Sūtras of Patañjali; Thorsons (2002); commentary on yoga sūtra 1.23; p. 78.

119. Swami Tapasyananda, Swami Nikhilananda. Śri Sarada Devi, the Holy Mother; Life and Conversations; Sri Ramakrishna Math; p. 301.

120. B.K.S. Iyengar. Light on the Yoga Sūtras of Patañjali; Thorsons (2002); p. 81-82.

121. Who Am I? The Teachings of Bhagavan Sri Ramana Maharshi; Sri Ramanasramam Tiruvannamalai (2010); p. 29-30.

122. Swami Sivananda. Japa Yoga: A Comprehensive treatise on Mantra-Sastra; The Divine Life Society 15th ed (2014); p.55.

123. Who Am I? The Teachings of Bhagavan Sri Ramana Maharshi; Sri Ramanasramam Tiruvannamalai (2010); p. 30.

124. The Bhagavad Gītā Text, Word-to-Word Meaning Translation and Commentary by Swami Sivananda; The Divine Life Society 11th ed (2003); Chapter 4, commentary to Verse 18; p. 88-89.

125. Swami Tapasyananda, Swami Nikhilananda. Śri Sarada Devi, the Holy Mother; Life and Conversations; Sri Ramakrishna Math; p. 344

Third Limb: Āsanas (Seat/Postures)

126. The Bhagavad Gītā Text, Word-to-Word Meaning Translation and Commentary by Swami Sivananda; The Divine Life Society 11th ed (2003); Chapter 5, commentary to Verse 15; p. 112.

127. Swami Sivananda. Vedanta for Beginners; The Divine Life Society 6th ed (2016); p. 66.

128. B.K.S. Iyengar. Light on the Yoga Sūtras of Patañjali; Thorsons (2002); p. 116.

129. Swami Sivananda. The Moksha Gita Commentary by Swami Krishnananda; The Divine Life Society eBook edition; p. 73.

Fourth Limb: Prāṇāyāma (Control of Vital Energy)

130. B.K.S. Iyengar. Light on the Yoga Sūtras of Patañjali; Thorsons (2002); p. 166-7.

131. B.K.S. Iyengar. Light on the Yoga Sūtras of Patañjali; Thorsons (2002); p. 87.

132. Swami Sivananda. Japa Yoga: A Comprehensive treatise on Mantra-Sastra; The Divine Life Society 15th ed (2014); p.91.

Fifth Limb: Pratyāhāra (Withdrawal of the Senses)

133. B.K.S. Iyengar. Light on the Yoga Sūtras of Patañjali; Thorsons (2002); p. 168.

134. Swami Vishnu-Devananda. Meditation and Mantras, Motilal Banarsidass Publishers 6th ed (2013); p. 186-7.

Sixth Limb: Dhāraṇā (Concentration)

135. Swami Sivananda. Thought Power; The Divine Life Society 15th ed (2007); p. 28.

Seventh Limb: Dhyāna (Meditation)

136. Swami Sivananda. The Moksha Gita; The Divine Life Society e-book; commentary to Chapter 6, verse 10; p. 75.

137. The Bhagavad Gītā Text, Word-to-Word Meaning Translation and Commentary by Swami Sivananda; The Divine Life Society 11th ed (2003); Chapter 6, commentary to Verse 12; p. 133.

138. Swami Venkatesananda. Vāsiṣṭha's Yoga; State University of New York Press (1993); p. 379.

139. Swami Sivananda. Brahma Sūtras; The Divine Life Society 4th ed (2008); Chapter IV Section 1 Topic 1; p. 476.

140. Swami Nikhilananda. Self-Knowledge of Sri Sankaracarya; Sri Ramakrishna Math (2015); p. 100-101.

141. Self-Enquiry of Bhagavan Sri Ramana Maharshi; Sri Ramanasramam Tiruvannamalai (1990).

142. Swami Sivananda. Brahma Sūtras; The Divine Life Society 4th ed (2008); Chapter IV Section 1 Topic 2; p. 477.

143. Swami Sivananda. Brahma Sūtras; The Divine Life Society 4th ed (2008); Chapter IV Section 1 (Topic 2) verse 3 commentary; p. 477.

144. Swami Sivananda. Bliss Divine; The Divine Life Society 10th ed (2017); p. 337.

145. Swami Nikhilananda. Self-Knowledge of Sri Sankaracarya; Sri Ramakrishna Math (2015); p. 107.

146. Swami Sivananda. Concentration & Meditation; The Divine Life Society 16th ed (2017); p. 110.

Eighth Limb: Samādhi (Absorption in Brahman)

147. Swami Sivananda. The Moksha Gita; The Divine Life Society e-book; verse VII.28; p. 108.

148. B.K.S. Iyengar. Light on the Yoga Sūtras of Patañjali; Thorsons (2002); p. 52.

149. *http://sivanandaonline.org/public_html/?cmd=displaysection§ion_id=884*

150. Swami Sivananda. The Moksha Gita; The Divine Life Society e-book; commentary to Chapter VI, verse 10; p. 76-7.

151. Swami Sivananda. The Moksha Gita; The Divine Life Society e-book; commentary to Chapter VI, verse 10; p. 75-6.

152. Swami Sivananda. The Moksha Gita; The Divine Life Society e-book; commentary to Chapter VI, verse 9; p. 74.

153. Swami Nikhilananda. Self-Knowledge of Sri Sankaracarya; Sri Ramakrishna Math (2015); p. 115.

154. Swami Vishnu-Devananda. Meditation and Mantras, Motilal Banarsidass Publishers 6th ed (2013); p. 207.

155. B.K.S. Iyengar. Light on the Yoga Sūtras of Patañjali; Thorsons (2002); p. 76.